Santa's Secret

A Story of Hope

Santa's Secret

A Story of Hope

*The True Story of America's
Secret Santa*

By Donna McGuire

World 2 Publishing

*Dedicated to Secret Santas everywhere
and in memory of a true gentleman,
John "Buck" O'Neil*

Published by World 2 Publishing, LLC
4243 N.E. Port Drive, Suite 1000, Lee's Summit, Missouri, 64064.
www.secretsantabook.com E-mail: info@secretsantabook.com

Edited by Sheila Davis
Cover art by David A. Thompson
Inside art by Cesily Lesko

The author thanks Ted Horn, Ray Wynn, George Hailey, Greg and Sarah
Lesko, Rick Taylor and Mainline Printing for contributions to this book.

Secret Santa thanks his friends who have served as elves and all the local, state
and federal law enforcement officials who guided his sleigh along the way.

Library of Congress Control Number: 2006936853

ISBN 0-9790248-0-1

Printed in the United States of America

First Edition

One

A Kansas City miracle

Fear gripped Kris Miller as he reached for the telephone Christmas Eve morning. He prayed the police could help him.

His wife and two stepsons were stranded at the Greyhound bus terminal in Kansas City, waiting on a connecting bus to Fort Smith, Arkansas. It wouldn't arrive until well after dark — more than 12 hours after Cimeri and the road-weary children had disembarked there.

That's not what worried Kris, though.

Strangers trolling that far-away building had talked the 25-year-old Cimeri into doing something crazy. Stuck in California, half a continent away, Kris felt powerless to protect her.

Just minutes earlier, he'd been talking to her as she stood at a bank of pay phones overlooking the bus bay. Though they had argued days earlier, they now ached to be with each other. Tears streaked Cimeri's cheeks. They had no money for return tickets after she and the boys visited her dad for Christmas. How would they get home?

Blake, her 2-year-old, sat quietly in a stroller beside her. Zachary, her 4-year-old, played an arcade game in the corner. About a dozen other travelers sprawled on terminal benches. Two employees took orders behind the concessions counter while others worked the ticket booth across the lobby.

The group of strangers entered. After briefly wandering past other bus riders, stopping to chat with a few, they walked toward Cimeri and huddled around her. The tallest stranger, a plump man clad in white overalls and a red flannel shirt, spoke briefly and waved money

1

before her, urging, "Put the phone down for a minute."

He towered over the petite Cimeri. Bewildered, she slowly lowered the receiver and looked into his blue eyes. What did he want?

At the other end of the phone, Kris strained to hear. He yelled for Cimeri to pick up the receiver, but she didn't respond.

A minute or two passed. Kris stewed. Finally, Cimeri's voice returned.

"Santa Claus just came and gave me $500," she said. "I'll have to call you right back."

Click.

One minute stretched to two, five and then 10. Kris grew nervous.

He called the Greyhound station. Cimeri and the boys had left, officials there said. Secret Santa took them away.

Panic stabbed Kris. Had this stranger kidnapped his family? Had he used money to lure them to the streets?

Kris called the Kansas City Police Department.

Yes, the city had a Secret Santa who gave away money, the police said. But they knew nothing of events at the bus station.

This can't be happening, Kris thought.

He dialed his father-in-law in Arkansas. Raymond Parks last talked to Cimeri earlier that morning. No, she hadn't called recently.

Kris told Raymond what had happened. Raymond gasped. Thousands of miles apart, both men worried as they waited to hear something — anything — from Cimeri.

At that moment, Cimeri and the boys sat inside a leather-trimmed luxury sport utility vehicle barreling south toward the Country Club Plaza, a shopping and restaurant mecca known as one of Kansas City's crown jewels. Santa and a man who said he was the Jackson County sheriff rode up front. The sheriff didn't wear a uniform, but he wore a badge and carried a gun.

A van with more strangers trailed the SUV.

Cimeri had no idea where her luggage was. Someone had put Blake's stroller in the second van. Surrounded by strangers, she had every right to be scared.

Yet the second van carried two Kansas City firefighters. Their uniforms comforted Cimeri. So did the business card she clutched in her hand. It was from a newspaper reporter following Santa, taking notes and pictures as he gave away money.

To Cimeri, the strangers represented an answer to her prayers. She felt safe. *Everything is going to be okay,* she thought. For her, an incredible journey was beginning.

The unfolding excursion warmed Santa's heart, too.

The night before, he prayed to meet someone special needing help on Christmas Eve. He often said such prayers at Christmas, his favorite time of the year.

Cimeri had answered his prayer.

§ § §

A day earlier, Santa gave $1,000 each to two families that firefighters helped him surprise at a fire station. One family recently had buried a daughter who'd been shot at random while riding in a car to work. The other family included a paramedic father who had missed weeks of work while recovering from health problems.

Christmas Eve morning Santa headed out again, looking for more ways to dish out dozens of Ben Franklins, his favorite Christmas cash.

The day broke clear but cold, much like the day before, when the thermometer never escaped the teens. The chill cut through Santa's red flannel shirt every time he approached a "target," as he called recipients.

Accompanied by several elves who met him at his house, Santa rendezvoused with the firefighters on Kansas City's east side. In two vehicles, they trolled Truman Road, a main east-west thoroughfare that cut through aging business districts and frayed neighborhoods. They stopped at a thrift store and later helped a man riding a bicycle and another man digging through trash on a street corner.

Jackson County Sheriff Tom Phillips, who began providing security for Santa more than a decade earlier, when he was a captain, steered the SUV. Lacking a specific destination, he operated under a simple plan: Look for people who look like they need help.

The elves scanned side streets and sidewalks, shouting if they saw anyone who fit the description.

After reaching downtown, Sheriff Tom circled a block near a homeless shelter. No one stirred. He turned north and cruised past the old Greyhound station, a hulk of a concrete building now empty. Santa noticed the shuttered facade and bolted upright.

"I came into Kansas City there," he said, almost to himself.

He looked around.

"Where's the new bus station?" he asked in a louder, excited voice.

After waiting at red lights and turning a couple of corners, Sheriff Tom located it a few blocks east. Smaller than the old terminal, it offered limited parking in front, near a drop-off lane where taxicabs idled. Large picture windows overlooked the bus bay on the north side.

Sheriff Tom pulled in and parked. Santa bounded from the SUV. The elves followed like puppies swarming their mother's heels.

Sheriff Tom stationed himself near the front door and scanned the lobby for potential trouble. If he saw something that worried him, he would wave off Santa.

Santa, meanwhile, introduced himself to the manager and explained that he wanted to give away cash.

§ § §

Married nearly two years, Cimeri and Kris recently had experienced rocky times. Cimeri decided it best to take the boys and stay with her dad for a time outside Fort Smith, a city of roughly 80,000 in western Arkansas.

Her father had been fighting heart and other problems. He lived alone in a house worth $44,000. Retired and on a fixed income, he could use Cimeri's help and longed to see his grandchildren. She lacked travel money, so he scraped together $440 for the tickets plus extra for suitcases and food. Cimeri picked up the cash from her sister, who also lived in California and shared a bank account with their dad.

At 3:30 p.m. December 22, Cimeri and the children climbed aboard a bus in Sacramento. Cimeri's niece told her, "When your babies get to sleep, pray that everything will work out."

Along the way, Cimeri prayed. But she doubted God listened.

Their route wound through Reno, Salt Lake City and Denver before turning east for a long straight overnight stretch across Kansas.

During the night, the bus broke down. Ice formed on the windows as passengers sat and waited. Huddled with Zachary and Blake, Cimeri worried about reaching Kansas City in time for the 7:45 a.m. bus to Fort Smith.

Sure enough, they arrived 10 minutes too late. Already tired of buses and terminals, they were to be stranded nearly all of Christmas Eve in a terminal.

Cimeri walked to the pay phones and called her dad to let him know they wouldn't arrive until about 3 a.m. Christmas morning. Later, she bought the boys an early lunch at the concession counter. Then, after watching another mother with three children spill their food as their bus was to leave, Cimeri gave her boys' food away.

She had about $10 left.

Still upset at her husband, she hadn't called Kris during the trip. Now she decided to at least let her mother-in-law know that she and the boys were okay. She walked to the pay phones again and dialed.

Cimeri's mother-in-law picked up. "Kris wants to talk to you," she said before putting him on the phone.

"I miss you," he cooed.

Cimeri melted.

She longed for home. Her anger with Kris faded. Her love for him soared.

Kris, a concrete laborer, relied on seasonal jobs and lacked money for bus tickets. He could drive to Arkansas, but there wasn't room for all of them in his truck, their only vehicle. Perhaps they both could work and save, and maybe he could come to Arkansas to pick them up in March or April in another vehicle.

Cimeri sobbed. That sounded like forever.

One of Santa's elves spotted Cimeri, grabbed Santa's arm and pointed.

"She's crying," the elf said.

Santa nodded. He'd get her last, on the way out.

"Don't let her leave," he said.

He walked through the waiting area, spreading bills to people waiting for buses to Chicago, Topeka, Mississippi and elsewhere. One thankful recipient bowed his head and made the sign of the cross.

Santa turned toward Cimeri. He offered $200 as she talked to Kris. She tried to wave him off, but Santa insisted and asked her to put down the phone for a minute. He leaned close and spoke softly.

"I came here in 1971 on a Greyhound bus, with $18 in my pocket and everything that I owned in one suitcase."

Cimeri's eyes widened. She reached for the $200.

"How many children do you have?" Santa asked.

"Two," she answered, gazing at Blake in the stroller.

Santa peeled off three more bills. That gave Cimeri $500, more than enough for tickets. Cimeri slapped her quivering chin, rubbed her moist eyes, spoke briefly to Kris and hung up the phone. More tears burst from her eyes.

She spilled her story — of missing her bus, of craving to see her dad, of having no money to get home.

Santa walked a few feet away, his mind spinning.

"We're going to get her to Arkansas," he said.

He pulled a cell phone from a pocket and dialed.

§ § §

Minutes passed as Santa paced. He wanted to put Cimeri and the boys on a commercial flight to Fort Smith, roughly 250 miles away. But it was Christmas Eve. Snagging one ticket was difficult. Snagging three on the same flight? Impossible.

As he sought a solution, Santa got another idea. He'd send Cimeri home after Christmas, too. He walked back toward her and announced that he'd buy her airplane tickets to California.

Her mouth fell open.

"You have to be a religious man," Cimeri said.

Santa recoiled in surprise.

"How did you know that?" he asked.

"Because people just don't do that," she said.

Cimeri said her dad was a retired preacher and that, during stops on the trip, every time she called her sister back in California, her sister told her to pray.

"You came along," Cimeri told Santa, "and I got some faith back."

Santa's eyes twinkled.

By now, though, Santa had broken one of his rules. He'd stayed too long in one place. A clerk at the concession stand had called at least one friend and advised: "Get over here. Santa is giving out money."

Santa needed to bolt. Yet a woman with two young children carrying a handful of hundred-dollar bills in a bus terminal would make an easy target. He couldn't abandon Cimeri.

"We're getting you out of here," he said.

One of Santa's elves grabbed the baby stroller. Another gently reached for Zachary. Cimeri scooped up Blake. They dashed outside and into the two vehicles.

At a Plaza restaurant, Santa rendezvoused with a man using the code name Noble Smith, who lived in nearby Miami County, Kansas. Santa was training him to become a Secret Santa, too. As the group waited for sandwiches, Fire Captain Ray Wynn, who doubles as an elf, made some phone calls. He hung up from one and grinned.

"I've got a pilot," he announced.

About the same time, Noble clicked off a call on his cell phone. "I've got a limousine driver," he said.

They turned to Cimeri. Which did she want? A private plane or a limo?

Speechless, she stared at her food and shrugged.

The others settled on the limousine.

Cimeri realized she hadn't called Kris back. Someone handed her a cell phone.

"They're taking me in a limousine to Arkansas," she blurted, "and then they are going to fly me home."

She paused.

"I'm serious."

Another pause.

"Yes, the sheriff is here — and firemen. I'm okay. They all have badges. Everything is legit. I'm coming home, honey. Me and the boys are coming home."

Half an hour later, outside the restaurant, Secret Santa handed Cimeri and the children off to Noble. For a fleeting moment, Cimeri felt nervous. This person hadn't been at the terminal, and the man who'd given her $500 and all those promises was leaving. Yet she buckled the children in the back seat and climbed in the front.

Noble provided crayons and coloring books and cookies and movies for their long ride. Inside his limousine, the children drifted to sleep.

Part way there, Cimeri called her dad.

"You're okay then?" he asked.

"Yes."

"I can't talk right now," he said, handing the phone to a relative.

He bawled.

Raymond Parks hadn't believed in Santa Claus for 55 years. Now, he did.

Hours later, Cimeri and her dad reunited at a Wal-Mart parking lot and fell into each other's arms, crying. On the way home, Raymond told Cimeri something he'd been afraid to say on the phone because he was afraid she wouldn't come: His house had burned down less than two weeks earlier, after a heater caught the wall on fire while he was away. He'd lost everything.

They headed to his sister's three-bedroom trailer home. Five adults and four children settled down for the night.

Christmas morning arrived. Despite the fire gloom and tight quarters, they felt determined to make Christmas cheerful.

That afternoon, a fire truck rumbled up the drive. A chief from the local volunteer fire department climbed off and delivered a message: Secret Santa had named Cimeri's dad as a special angel. Along with the award, Raymond would receive a $1,000 check, the chief said.

Raymond started crying again.

"It was just hard for me to accept," he said later. "I never had to be on the receiving end, I was always on the giving end for years."

He considered Santa a blessing.

"They can call him Secret Santa, they can call him an angel, but I call him a messenger from God. That was God-sent."

Four days after Christmas, longing for home, Cimeri and the boys boarded a Northwest Airlines flight carrying tickets from Santa. Their itinerary: Fort Smith to Memphis to Minneapolis to Sacramento.

She believed in prayer again.

"I believe in miracles, too," she said. "I never thought one would happen to me."

§ § §

Some say it took many miracles for Santa to be able to help Cimeri and hundreds of others.

Friends who know his childhood story say he had every reason and excuse to fail. His mother, unable to keep him, left him to be raised by his impoverished grandparents in a small Mississippi town where others considered him white trash. His father never visited.

Even as a young man, poverty clung to his heels. Once homeless himself, he nearly turned to petty crime. But he didn't.

A self-made millionaire, Santa has given more than $1.3 million to needy families during more than a quarter-century handing out Christmas cash, all without the benefit of a tax deduction. He's operated mostly in Kansas City but also in New York, California, Florida and elsewhere.

Some folks, including the homeless who congregate downtown, call him the "hundred-dollar bill man." Others who've seen his story on television or read about him in the newspaper call him Secret Santa.

Selected media who tag along agree not to show Santa's face or reveal his identity. As long as they keep this promise, they can follow him a few hours each Yuletide and retell heart-warming stories. They record a snippet of his work.

Santa often spends several days searching. He finds some recipients through tips from law enforcement officers, social service agencies or firefighters. Others he nabs simply by trolling downtrodden neighborhoods.

He has a knack for spotting people down on their luck: drivers of rusted cars, the elderly walking several blocks to the store, moms washing clothes at a coin-operated laundry, parents lugging old microwaves or worn televisions to a pawn shop so they can buy Christmas gifts for the kids.

How did he reach this point?

When Santa looks back, he doesn't focus on the excuses he had to fail. He embraces something else.

He embraces a story of hope.

Two

A fearful prayer

I t was time to go, his grandmother announced. Her 5-year-old grandson slid his small hand into his grandmother's warm palm and looked expectantly at his grandfather, who pushed himself up from his favorite chair. They ambled out the front door for a 20-minute walk to the Baptist church, where a somber crowd gathered.

His grandfather, lanky yet muscular, towered nearly a foot-and-a-half above his grandmother, who'd stopped growing while still an inch shy of 5 feet. They'd already sent six grown children into the world. Now they were raising one of their grandchildren, the blue-eyed boy who would become Secret Santa.

Walking between them, Santa hustled each step to keep up with the longer-legged adults as they trudged up a hill and past the Church of Christ through a neighborhood of nicer homes to a spot where the red brick church came into view. Cars toting families flowed into the parking lot. Ushers stood at the doors.

Inside, Santa slipped into a pew between his grandparents and looked around at people waving cardboard fans in front of their reddened faces. Sweat beaded on foreheads and pasted hair to damp necks.

Up front, a casket held the body of a man who was both father and husband. Some people wept. Others dabbed moist eyes with handkerchiefs.

Many children, some smaller than Santa, squirmed in pews alongside their parents. Eventually, the crowd hushed. A hymn began. Voices rose in unison.

Later, the preacher talked about the man in the casket. More people cried.

On the way home, Santa asked what had happened. His grandmother explained that the man in the casket had gone to heaven to be with Jesus.

Santa pondered this. What about the man's wife and children? What were they going to do now? Why did God take the man away from them? The man was a lot younger than Santa's grandparents, both born in 1881 and already past 70 years old.

A horrible thought overcame Santa. If that man could die, so could his grandparents. His stomach felt like mush.

Shortly after they reached home, Santa bolted and ran down a little hill — not much more than a bank of red clay, really — to his special hiding place. Standing there, near two pine trees, he could see just the top of the house.

Clasping his hands tightly, he prayed.

"Please, God. Don't take Pa and Mama away. Please."

They were the only parents he'd ever known. He shook at the thought of losing them.

His mother had gotten pregnant in another state, come to her parents' home to give birth then returned to her husband in Tennessee. Her husband's name appeared on Santa's birth certificate as his father, but Santa found it strange that he never visited or wrote. His mother came sometimes, but not all that often. His birth parents didn't feel like parents to him.

What if his grandparents died? What would happen? He shuddered.

Santa trudged back up the hill to the house, hopped on the porch and went inside, letting the screen door slam. His grandfather looked up from his chair and frowned.

The prayer had done little to ease Santa's fears, but for now that was all he could do. He sat and watched his grandmother rinse vegetables in the kitchen.

They lived in the small north-central Mississippi town where his grandparents had settled after the Great Depression. Founded after the turn of the century, the town sat at the junction of county cross-roads. It boasted a general store, two grocery stores, a pool hall and saw mill. Railroad tracks running east and west served as an unofficial but respected housing boundary. White folks lived on the north side, black folks on the south.

Many adults worked for the saw mill, picked cotton or farmed. Others owned the land, ran businesses or taught school.

Santa and his grandparents shared a small white house with a green shingled roof. It had a front room, kitchen, eating area and two small bedrooms, but no bathroom. The kitchen faucet carried only cold water. For hot water, his grandmother heated a kettle on the wood-burning stove.

At bathing time, his grandparents carried a large galvanized tub into the kitchen. They poured hot water from the stove in first, fol-lowed by enough cold water to lower the temperature to the bather's liking.

When it rained, the roof leaked. His grandmother saved coffee cans and knew just where to position them to catch the dripping water. Sometimes, her eight or 10 cans weren't enough and she employed a kitchen bowl, too. Santa's heart beat fast when thunder shook the heavens.

In winter, the fireplace warmed the front room, which at night became the bedroom. His grandparents slept near the door; Santa curled up on a rollaway bed in one corner. If the weather grew espe-cially cold, his grandmother ironed the sheets before bedtime. She piled on the homemade quilts. They had no furnace.

In the summer, Mississippi's soaring heat and stifling humidity made sleeping uncomfortable. Flies and mosquitoes found their way through a hole in the screen door and buzzed past Santa's ears.

The two small bedrooms usually were reserved for the aunts, uncles and cousins who occasionally visited.

When nature called, Santa trudged to the outhouse, perhaps 200 feet from the back door, past the garden. At one time the outhouse had borne a fresh coat of paint, but the years had stripped the color until only battered wood remained. In the winter, when the temperature often dipped into the 30s at night, they used a "slop jar" – Santa's name for a chamber pot. One of the chores Santa disliked most was emptying the slop jars in the mornings.

His grandmother kept house, canned vegetables and fixed their meals. She washed clothes by immersing them in soapy water and rubbing them against a washboard in an old tub out back. After rinsing, she fed them through a wringer on the back porch before hanging them to dry.

His grandfather plowed gardens, picked cotton and sometimes cut timber for the saw mill, a bustling venture that benefited from acres and acres of woods. He often carried his lunch, fixed by grandmother, in a molasses bucket.

Extremely strong, usually quiet and poorly educated, grandfather had been a share cropper as a young man and saved enough to buy a small farm, but he lost it during the Depression. That was the only property Santa's grandparents ever owned. One of their children had purchased the house in which they now lived with Santa.

Many evenings, grandfather clicked on the small plastic radio that sat in the front room, which was lighted dimly by one bulb dangling from the ceiling. Some nights, music from the Grand Ole Opry in Nashville squawked from the box. Other nights, they caught a drama or comedy, such as "The Shadow," "The Green Hornet" or "Fibber McGee and Molly." Santa enjoyed "The Lone Ranger" and "Gunsmoke" the most. On fall Saturdays, grandfather sometimes tuned in the Ole Miss Rebels football games called by play-by-play announcer Charles Sullivan. Since grandmother hated football, grandfather turned on games only when she was busy outside.

Grandfather also plucked the banjo, and grandma played the fiddle. Santa picked up a love of music from them. Many Saturday afternoons, they strolled to the feed store for some merriment, often teaming with another musician on a guitar. Many in the crowd danced. Sometimes, someone shouted square-dance calls. On those days, Santa scampered up in the corner on feed sacks to watch, mesmerized by the happy and whirling scene.

One of grandfather's passions was "trade day," the first Monday of each month at a neighboring county seat. Traders came from miles around. One day, grandfather spotted a plow horse that he favored. The owner feared the horse was moon-eyed, meaning it was either blind or semi-blind. Grandfather suspected a temporary affliction. He offered a Barlow pocket knife for the horse. Everyone knew that Barlow made good knives. Even Mark Twain referred to a Barlow in "The Adventures of Tom Sawyer" and "The Adventures of Huckleberry Finn."

The swap made, the former horse owner thought he'd gotten the better of grandfather. Turns out, the opposite was true. The horse, named Babe, soon healed and helped grandfather earn a little money plowing gardens.

Santa liked watching grandfather follow the muscular horse as the plow broke fresh ground. Grasping the leather reins, grandfather yelled, "Gee-haw," and directed Babe straight down the rows.

When asked what he wanted for his fifth birthday, Santa blurted that he wanted to plow Babe like grandfather did. One spring day grandfather granted his wish. Santa grabbed the reins and took his place behind the heavy turning plow, nearly as big as he was. At grandfather's command old Babe took off. The heavy plow toppled over.

"Whoa!" grandfather yelled before righting the plow and setting Santa off again, only to watch the plow plop once more. Down inside, grandfather laughed as the little guy tried to do a big man's job, but grandfather hid his amusement, not wanting to humiliate the boy.

Their garden stretched 150 by 200 feet. As spring blended into summer, strawberries, green beans, turnip greens, collards, cabbage, corn, watermelon, okra and tomatoes sprouted and ripened. Santa loved the strawberry patch and sometimes endured grandmother's scolding for eating figs off the fig tree before they were ripe.

His grandparents journeyed regularly to the nearby county seat to collect commodities, such as peanut butter, oats, cheese, powdered milk and dried beans. If they were lucky, they got powered eggs and molasses, too. Sometimes they rode in a wagon behind Babe. Other times, they hitched a ride with someone.

As summer faded into autumn, cotton ripened. One day, grandmother handed young Santa a cotton bag she'd sewn him out of a flour sack so he could help pick the fluffy white puffs from atop their prickly pods. He slung the shoulder harness over his head, letting the bag hang to one side. For him, the cotton stood about eye-high. Before long, Santa lost interest in picking and fell asleep in the warm sun, curled between rows of cotton. The adults looked at him and smiled, wishing they could join him. Instead, they continued to toil, their hands bleeding, to earn a penny a pound.

Santa didn't realize they were poor until he started school. Other children wore better clothes and newer shoes. They owned toys, played with pets and rode in cars. Their homes had indoor bathrooms, telephones and gas stoves.

They had lots of things Santa didn't have. They had different lives.

Three

Learning to cope

One day during first-grade recess, Santa picked up a hickory nut, cocked his arm and threw. The nut plunked the eye of another first-grader named Cecil, who began to bawl.

"I'm going to tell teacher on you!" Cecil squealed.

"You don't tell," Santa said, quickly trying to think of a way to avoid punishment, "and I'll bring you a big bag of candy tomorrow."

Cecil thought this over. His eye stung, but that much candy sounded good.

"Okay," he said.

Santa had no candy at home. And he couldn't ask his grandparents to buy him a bagful.

The next day, Cecil demanded: "Where's my candy?"

"Oh," Santa said, "I forgot. I'll bring it tomorrow."

The following day, Cecil spouted the same question. Santa gave the same answer. This lasted more than a month. Eventually, Cecil forgot to ask about the candy.

§ § §

As the first-graders grew and advanced to older grades, friendships formed. With friendships came invitations to other children's homes for weekend play, overnight stays or birthday parties.

Ashamed of his grandparents' home, Santa didn't invite anyone to his house. If any of his friends came by to play, he stayed outside with them.

He figured other ways to cope, too.

When his friends talked at school about what they had watched on television the previous day — such as "Sky King," "The Adventures of Rin Tin Tin" and "Howdy Doody" — Santa looked at the ground, digging his toe into the dirt. He didn't want his friends to know that his family didn't have a television.

One evening, he climbed onto a neighbor's porch and watched their television through a window. Since the window was open, he could hear dialogue, too. The next day at school, he joined the conversation about television.

He returned to the neighbor's porch several times, especially when "The Millionaire" came on with Michael Anthony. Each episode, the millionaire cut a million-dollar cashier's check and delivered it to some lucky house in America. It was fiction, not real, but Santa didn't know that. He used to pray, "Oh Lord, let it be our house this time." Of course, it never was.

Santa always let the neighbors know when he arrived on the porch, either by whistling or clearing his throat.

"You want to come inside and watch TV?" Mrs. Rogers would ask.

"No, I'm fine," Santa answered.

Mrs. Rogers turned up the volume.

§ § §

One morning, Santa slipped his foot into his right shoe and felt the hole in the sole. It had been there before, patched by his grandmother with cardboard. Now it was back. Only bigger.

"Mama!" Santa called out, holding up the shoe for her to see.

She grabbed her scissors, cut another piece of cardboard and pressed it inside the shoe. Santa slipped it on, tied the shoestring and headed out the door, watchful of puddles. Wet cardboard crumbled into a soggy mess.

To make sure others didn't see the holes, Santa shuffled as he walked, keeping his feet close to the ground. One day, though, he got distracted, forgot to shuffle and exposed the hole to a schoolmate standing behind him.

"Oh, look!" the boy teased. "You've got holes in your shoes. Ha, ha, ha."

Santa clenched his jaw.

A few weeks later, after the hole expanded, Santa discovered on his way to school that the cardboard had worn out again. Halfway to school, he ditched his shoes and proceeded barefoot even though it was winter.

"Where are your shoes?" a classmate asked.

"I'm so tough I don't need shoes," he said.

The next couple of days, four or five of his friends came to school barefooted. They wanted to show how tough they were, too.

§ § §

One Saturday on the town square, Santa and others gathered near the grocery store to listen to a blind man play a guitar. Listeners dropped coins into a cup on the end of the guitar. A big man in the crowd stared at Santa. He knew that the boy lived with his grandparents, not his parents. He wondered why.

"Who's your daddy?" the man demanded.

Santa spit out his grandfather's name.

"Well, I know old-man Oscar, and he ain't your daddy. Who is your daddy?"

Santa again recited his grandfather's name. But the big man pushed harder, this time asking, "Who's your *real* daddy?"

Flustered, Santa blurted the name of the man married to his mother, the man listed on his birth certificate.

"He lives in Little Rock, Arkansas," Santa said defiantly.

"Oh, okay," the big man said, backing off.

Santa loved his grandparents, but he felt different, not having real parents like everyone else. He didn't know anyone else being raised by people so old.

§ § §

After each Christmas, Santa's classmates returned to school excitedly talking about the toys they'd received. Some wore new sweaters, pants and shoes.

"What did you get?" a child asked Santa one year.

Santa made up something grandiose.

The next day, the classmate asked Santa why he didn't bring his gift for show and tell.

"I forgot," Santa answered, using the same fib that worked with Cecil about the candy episode in first grade.

Grandmother had given Santa fruit for Christmas. He liked fruit, but other children got toys and clothes. Sure, one year he'd gotten a toy gun and a holster. That was really cool. Another time, he opened wrapping paper and found a pair of socks inside, something he really needed.

But to Santa, every Christmas should have been about toys and candy and other nifty goodies — things other children received. Santa's grandparents couldn't afford that.

Even their Christmas tree looked different. Each year, his grandfather cut a cedar tree from the woods. His grandmother hung the same four or five ornaments and recycled icicles on it. They had no lights for it.

§ § §

Feeling bored one warm summer day, Santa walked to the barn to see what Babe was doing. The sour smell of ripe feed filled Santa's nostrils.

The barn was small, not much more than a shed, really, with just enough room to protect Babe from heat or rain. Wooden planks to one side of the stall covered a storage area where grandfather kept Babe's feed.

Babe's leather collars hung from the wall, next to the leather reins grandfather used when he hitched Babe to the plow. The plow itself and other farm tools were stored around back, in what had been an old smokehouse.

Santa leaned against the barn door and watched Babe flick his tail to ward off flies biting his rump. It had been at least a couple of years since a 5-year-old Santa tried to follow Babe with the plow. Now, as he looked at the horse, another idea popped into his mind. Wouldn't it be fun to ride Babe?

He looked around. There was nothing to stand on so he could climb onto the horse's bare back. He spotted the wooden planks that made up the side of the storage area next to Babe. Santa scampered up the planks, using them like ladder rungs. When high enough, he turned and jumped onto the horse.

Babe jerked his head and bolted.

Immediately, Santa knew he'd made a mistake. As the horse raced outside, Santa grabbed for the rafter across the barn opening. Babe vanished, snorting and grunting. Hanging by his hands from the rafter, Santa looked down. It was a long drop. Should he yell for his grandmother? No, he would get a whuppin' if she found out.

He dropped to the dirt, landing hard. He stood up and dusted himself off. At least he wasn't hurt.

He never tried to ride Babe again.

§ § §

An athletic boy, Santa began playing peewee football in fourth grade. Since he didn't have his own uniform, he borrowed one from another boy who played on different days. That worked dandy the first year, but the next, Santa's game times conflicted with the other boy's team. Santa no longer could borrow the uniform. Without a uniform, he could not play.

Santa pondered what to do. One day, while thumbing through the Sears & Roebuck catalog, he stopped on a page that pictured a helmet, shoulder pads, jersey and pants. Santa stared and stared. *Oh man, look at that!*

He knew that Sears shipped before requiring payment. Maybe he'd just order the uniform and figure out how to pay later. He could sell greeting cards, cut grass, rack tables at the pool hall — whatever it took. Yup, he just had to order that uniform.

His finger turned more pages and his eyes lit upon a Winchester rifle. Not a real rifle, but a gun that shot caps. It looked real, though. It wasn't much more money, he figured. At least, it didn't seem like that much. He ordered the uniform and the gun.

He told his coach he'd have his uniform by the first game. He grew excited thinking about it.

But as game day approached, Santa continued to wait on Sears & Roebuck. Panic gnawed his chest. The thought of missing the game unnerved him. For days, he'd walked to the Post Office and asked, "Do you have a package?"

"Nope," the clerk always answered. "Don't have a package."

So this day, the final day of mail before the game, he prayed as hard as he'd ever prayed, asking God for the uniform to arrive. Then he trudged to the Post Office, stepped inside and walked to the counter.

"Do you have a package?" Santa asked in a pleading voice.

"Nope," came the answer. "Don't have a package."

Santa's cheeks flushed. He raced out the door as tears formed in his eyes and curled down his cheeks. He was a boy, and he wasn't supposed to cry. He wiped his cheeks dry.

He walked head down, brooding and kicking rocks. After he reached his yard, he remembered that sometimes a late batch of mail arrived just before the Post Office closed each day.

He fell to his knees in his grandparents' garden, near the pole beans.

"Oh Lord, please let it be there," he prayed.

He wandered back to the Post Office and hung around until he knew it was late enough for the late mail. He went inside and looked up at the clerk.

"You know," the clerk said, rubbing his chin, "I've had some mail come in. Hold on."

Santa shifted his weight from foot to foot, waiting.

The clerk returned carrying two packages, one quite large.

Santa scurried home and sneaked into the yard through the back, by the garden. He ripped open the packages. One contained his cap rifle, which he hid under a pile of bean poles. The other contained the uniform. He tried on the helmet. It fit.

Since Santa had brought his friend's uniform home many times the previous year, his grandmother didn't question whose uniform this was. Santa felt so proud, he wanted to wear it to school.

The bill stunned grandmother. She called her grandson to the kitchen and demanded to know why he'd done such a thing. After telling him he'd have to help earn the money to pay the bill, she admonished him again.

"Don't do that anymore," she said sternly.

Santa's ears turned red. He hated upsetting his grandparents.

Alas, Sears & Roebuck also carried real go-carts powered by gasoline. One day, Santa spotted them in the catalog and couldn't take his eyes off one particular go-cart. His desire got the better of him.

This time, Sears & Roebuck delivered. When no one answered the delivery driver's knock, the driver walked to a neighbor's house and asked what to do. The neighbor knew that Santa's grandparents had gone to visit relatives. She called.

When his grandmother walked to the phone to take the call, Santa followed to listen.

"There's a truck here," the neighbor said. "They've got a delivery from Sears & Roebuck. It's a go-cart."

Grandmother turned to Santa.

"Did you order a go-cart?" she demanded.

A lump caught in his throat.

"No-o-o-o," he stammered. "I don't think so."

Grandma turned back to the phone. "They must be at the wrong place."

Relief washed over Santa. He didn't know how he ever would have paid for a go-cart.

§ § §

His grandparents kept chickens in an old chicken coop out back. As a youngster, Santa helped gather eggs. Some Sundays after church, as a special treat, grandmother grabbed an old rooster or hen and popped its neck off. The headless bird floundered a bit, soon to be plucked and fried.

Some time after they ran out of chickens, Santa found himself hankering for fried eggs. The powdered eggs his grandparents picked up at the county seat didn't taste nearly as good as fresh eggs.

As he sat on the porch one summer night with his grandparents, Santa noticed that the breeze once again carried with it the rank smell of chicken dung. It blew from across the dirt road, where neighbors tended at least 100 chickens in a commercial chicken coop on a three-acre lot. On hot days, the smell worsened. After awhile, Santa grew used to it.

The chickens lived in wire cages and laid eggs onto a platform built at a slant, so that eggs rolled into a trough from which they were gathered and sold. The owners also ran the seed and feed store in town.

One summer night, a friend of Santa's suggested they go to the "chicken store."

"What do you mean?" Santa asked.

His friend pointed across the street.

Late that night, they sneaked across the road in the dark and gathered as many eggs as they could carry. The chickens stirred. A few squawked, alerting the rest. A ruckus burst forth.

A door opened on a nearby house, where the son of the chicken coop owner lived. He shone a light on the coop from his porch and yelled, "Who's down there?"

Santa and his friend crouched in the dark, holding their breath as their hearts raced and they waited for the man to turn back inside.

"Does he have a gun?" Santa's friend asked.

Santa shrugged. He didn't know. He prayed they wouldn't get shot.

When they felt it was safe, the boys scampered back across the road.

Varying his route so as not to be detected, Santa returned to the "chicken store" several times that summer. He left eggs in the kitchen for his grandmother, who never asked where Santa got them. Santa figured she knew, though.

She had a way of finding out things.

SANTA'S SECRET: A STORY OF HOPE

.

Four

Something to prove

A young friend approached a 10-year-old Santa on the town square.

"Come with me," said the friend, a boy three years older than Santa. "Do what I tell you. We are going to make some money."

They walked to the drug store, which featured a soda fountain and also served as a gathering place for townsfolk. Two men played checkers near the front window. A clerk rang up purchases behind a counter.

"Sit over there," Santa's friend said, pointing to a stool near the door.

The friend wandered deeper inside. About 10 minutes later, he returned and motioned to Santa to get up.

"Let's go," he blurted.

They dashed outside and ran to a spot behind the theater, where they stopped, breathless. The friend looked around, making sure they weren't being watched, then reached under his shirt and pulled out a woman's pocketbook.

"Where did you get that?" Santa asked.

The friend glared at him. "Keep your mouth shut and do what I tell you to do," he said. He opened the pocketbook, grabbed its money and stuffed it into his pocket.

"Here," he said, handing Santa the pocketbook. "Take this and put it right out there on the sidewalk, by the bridge."

The pocketbook's owner crossed the bridge every day as she walked to work. She'd figure she dropped it, the friend reasoned, and someone would have taken the money before she found it again.

Santa looked up and down the street then dashed to the bridge, dropped the evidence and ran back to his friend.

They walked a few blocks to a cotton gin, where they stashed some of the money. They pocketed the rest and headed for the pool hall, one of Santa's favorite places. He could play for hours. They hadn't been there long when the door swung open and law enforcement officers entered. With steely eyes, they stared at Santa. His muscles tensed. He looked away and swallowed.

Uh, oh, he thought. *This looks like trouble.*

The officers corralled the boys, escorted them outside and began an interrogation.

"If you don't tell us the truth," one said, "then we are going to put you in reform school."

Santa's friend glared at them.

"I don't know what you are talking about," he told the officers. "You can't prove it."

Butterflies circled in Santa's stomach. His heart pounded. He knew what reform school meant and wanted no part of it.

Eventually, the officers separated the boys. Whatever resolve Santa had to remain silent evaporated. He sang like a mockingbird on a clear summer morning.

"Okay," one officer said. "Let's go."

They marched the boys back to the drug store to see Mrs. Barbee, the woman whose pocketbook they had taken. She'd lost $10 and change. She looked at them and shook her head.

"Don't you know how hard I have to work for this little bit of money?" she said in a firm but calm voice. "This is all I have to raise my children."

When she finished, an officer told the boys, "We are going to take you home now."

He looked at Santa and added, "And we will have to tell your grandparents."

The butterflies in Santa's stomach doubled. How could they? Tell

Pa and Mama? Oh, Lord. He was going to get a whuppin'.

"Please, no," Santa said. "I won't do it again."

His grandparents saw the patrol car pull up and grew concerned. An officer opened the door. Santa slid out, stared at the ground and said nothing.

The officers explained. Anger colored grandmother's face. Disappointment covered grandfather's. Santa looked up briefly. Their looks stung him worse than a switch to his backside could have.

For days, Santa couldn't look his grandfather in the eye. Instead, Santa stared at the floor or the ground.

Finally, his grandfather broke the silence.

"I know that you didn't set out to do that," he said. "I know you didn't set out to hurt Miss Barbee. That's over and done with. I don't think I'll ever have to worry about you doing that again."

"No, Pa," Santa answered. "I won't do that again."

§ § §

Several months later, grandfather took ill. He coughed and wheezed and wheezed and coughed. The sickness turned to pneumonia, which sapped the 77-year-old man even worse. His doctors shipped him many miles away to the veterans hospital in Jackson. Weeks passed.

Some days, when grandmother wasn't looking, Santa cried. What would happen to grandmother and him if grandfather died? Memories from the funeral he attended years earlier flooded back. His stomach turned to mush.

They had no phone to call grandfather, but occasionally the neighbor let them use hers. Other times, they sent letters through grandmother's nephew in Jackson. Grandfather never wrote back. Grandfather knew numbers well enough to add and subtract, but he couldn't write more than his name. He never got much schooling, having dropped out in the third grade.

The illness lingered. Santa's mother, who lived in Memphis, went to Jackson to see her father.

After five months, word came that the doctors were letting grandfather go home. Santa celebrated. His uncle and aunt came from Alabama in their 1953 Ford and picked up Santa and grandmother. They arrived in Jackson too late for visiting hours, so they spent the night with relatives. Santa tossed and turned all night.

When he saw grandfather the next morning, Santa gasped. The lanky man who had awed Santa with his strength looked thin and frail. His gait used to be filled with pep. Now, he barely moved. His muscles had been rippled. Now, everything about him looked soft and weak and *really, really* old.

The doctors said he needed plenty of rest.

They drove home and helped grandfather inside, where he eased himself into his recliner and smiled. It felt good to be home, grandfather said.

Even when grandfather felt well enough to tackle chores, others refused to let him. "You've got to rest," relatives told him. "You can't do this. You can't do that."

Grandmother scolded him, too.

"You just sit there," she said when he got up to do something. "I'll take care of that."

For months, their routine varied little. Grandfather sat in his recliner. He chatted with visitors. He watched grandmother work. He asked Santa how school was going or how the garden looked.

One Sunday morning, Santa raced inside from playing with his cousins, who were visiting from another town. Out of breath, he plopped in a chair.

"What you been doing?" his grandfather asked.

Santa started to answer but stopped when he saw grandfather gasp. Grandfather's body stiffened, his head tilted backward, his eyes rolled up. Air gushed from his lungs.

Santa screamed. His aunt raced in the room.

"Get the doctor!" she commanded.

They still didn't have a phone, as grandfather couldn't see paying for one just to talk to people. Santa raced out the front door, sprinted to the neighbors' house and pounded on their door. No one answered. He pounded louder. Nothing.

He turned toward the road and ran more than a mile to the hospital. He pushed open a door and, out of breath, told the nurses, "You've got to get the doctor."

Reached at home, the doctor said he'd get right over to Santa's house. Santa dashed back the way he'd come, praying along the way that grandfather would be okay.

When he entered the house, his heart sank.

The heart attack struck Aug. 9, 1959. Grandfather was 78.

Santa, who was 11, had watched grandfather take his last breath. Grandmother became a widow at age 77, after roughly 60 years of marriage.

The funeral took place Tuesday. Afterward, relatives returned to the house to share food and consolation. Santa's mother, the fifth of six children, joined her siblings. At one point, the adults gathered in the kitchen. One looked at Santa.

"Go outside," he said.

Santa trudged out the front door, letting the screen slam, and sneaked to the back porch to listen. He recognized his mother's shrill voice, which dominated the debate.

"He's my child," she told the others, "and he's coming to Memphis. I'm going to raise him."

"No," Santa's grandmother shot back. "You're not."

Sweat beaded on Santa's forehead.

The arguing escalated. Eventually, one of the men spoke.

"School will start soon," he said. "Maybe we could let the boy stay with his grandmother at least for a little while and see how things go."

Others sided with that uncle. His mother had lost.

Relief washed over Santa. He felt like yelling *Alleluia!*

§ § §

Around Christmas, grandmother slipped and fell. As she landed, a bone in her arm snapped. The relatives descended again. An uncle, whom Santa liked, offered to take in Santa and his grandmother, but Santa's mother refused. Her mother could go live in Alabama with J.W., she said, but not her boy.

"He's coming with me," she told them defiantly.

This time, she won.

He didn't want to go. He squealed and argued, but it didn't matter. He was off to Memphis, to a new school system in a new state.

His mother lived in a government housing project, which didn't help his transition. Santa missed his grandmother and his friends and his teacher and his quieter way of life.

The first day at his new school, he moped, hardly paying attention.

His second day, the class bully teased him and started a fight.

Nearly every day for the first two weeks, someone picked on Santa, the new kid from Mississippi. He had no friends. He longed to hang out with Cecil.

One day, the bully and his entourage surrounded Santa in the hall. The bully pressed in close, staring at Santa. Suddenly, he grabbed Santa and slammed him against the wall.

"Stop it!" Santa said, squirming to get free.

The bully and his friends laughed. The bully was older and bigger than his classmates. No one dared challenge him. He teased Santa some more, poked him in the stomach and let him go.

For days, Santa plotted to get even.

One day, toward the end of recess, Santa sneaked back into the building ahead of the other pupils. He knew the bully liked to be first in line. He also knew that anyone coming indoors from the playground took a few seconds to adjust to the dimmer hallway light. For a few seconds, it was as if they were blind. Santa figured he could use that to his advantage. So he slipped inside and waited.

When the bully entered, Santa reared back and punched him as hard as he could. Boom! The bully crashed to the floor. Santa looked down, triumphant.

The punch was born out of frustration, but it gained him respect. After that, he and the bully became friends. Soon, no one dared take on either of them.

Solving his home problems proved more difficult. Santa and his mother argued daily. He disliked her rules. She demanded he do what she told him.

One day, he erupted.

"I'm going back!" he yelled.

"No! You're not."

"I'm going to run away!"

"No you're not! I'll have the cops put you in jail."

And so it went.

At the end of the school year, while his mother worked, Santa called an old neighbor back in Mississippi.

"Hey," the neighbor said, "your Uncle Roy is here."

Uncle Roy was a hobo, through and through. One never knew when he might turn up or how long he might stay. Sometimes he'd hang around six weeks, sometimes a few days. He was a great blues guitar player who sometimes played the harmonica. Santa listened to him for hours. But Uncle Roy also drank heavily.

Santa begged the neighbor to put Uncle Roy on the phone. She fetched him. When he heard Uncle Roy's voice, Santa began to cry.

"I'm going to run off," he said, sobbing. "I'm going to catch a train."

"You can't do that," Uncle Roy said. "You never know where them trains are going to take you."

"Well, I'll find out. I'm running away."

Uncle Roy asked Santa not to do anything until he heard back from him. Santa agreed. They hung up.

Later that day, the phone rang. Uncle J.W. from Alabama was on the line. Santa told him he was going to run away, that he couldn't take it any longer.

"Don't do anything," said Uncle J.W., who still was caring for Santa's grandmother. "I'm coming to Memphis."

Late the next day, after Santa's mother arrived home from work, a knock came at the door. When his mother opened it, she saw her brother-in-law from Alabama.

"Come on in," she said, surprised. "Have you got some business in Memphis?"

"Yep, I sure do," he said. "I'm taking the boy with me and we are going home."

She stared at him. Her surprise turned to indignation.

"The boy is none of your business," she said.

Uncle J.W. argued, not gaining ground but not giving any, either. Santa stepped between them, looked his mother in the eye and scowled.

"You are *not* going to keep me in this house," he said, "because I *will* run away."

Uncle J.W. sighed.

"Let the boy go be with the only person he's known as his mother," he said, "and I'll be responsible for him."

"Take him, then," she said. She turned and walked away.

Santa packed quickly.

When they reached his uncle's home, Santa hugged his grandmother. He felt as if he had been released from prison. He knew he'd never go back to his mother.

If anything happened to grandmother, he'd go be a hobo with Uncle Roy.

§ § §

Before school began for the fall term in 1960, Uncle J.W. took Santa and his grandmother back to Mississippi. They moved into the old house. Uncle J.W. fixed the roof so it wouldn't leak anymore, though Santa still shuddered when it thundered.

Someone hooked up a washing machine on the back porch. Grandmother no longer had to use the old washboard.

Later, grandmother paid $20 for a used black-and-white television in a large console. They rigged an antenna on the roof and tuned in two channels, one rather fuzzy. When "Perry Mason" — grandmother's favorite show — came on, Santa wasn't allowed to make a sound.

Santa resumed his friendship with Cecil and turned his attention to athletics. Santa loved football and basketball. He had some athletic gifts but they were raw. One coach pushed him to "work hard, play hard and practice hard."

"If you would practice like you play in a game, there's no limit to what you can do," the coach insisted. "You can go to college on a scholarship."

"Really?" Santa asked. "You really think so?"

"You can play college football," the coach said. "I know you can."

High school started, and with it came football. Santa started his sophomore season as the first-string safety and fourth-string quarterback. As any fan knows, fourth-string quarterbacks are about as likely to get on the field as 5-foot-1 actors are to become leading men. Yet the first-string quarterback fumbled twice the first game. In came the second-string quarterback, who also fumbled.

Before the game ended, all four quarterbacks had played. In a brief appearance, Santa performed well enough — for a rookie. After that, Coach David Oakes took extra time to tutor him. A few games later, Santa jogged onto the field as the starting quarterback.

Grandmother never watched him play. She feared he would get hurt.

One day as Santa was leaving for a Friday night game, she implored him in a serious voice, "Now, honey, don't you let them hit you with that ball."

"Mama, I won't let them hit me with that ball," he answered, smiling to himself. He knew if she ever came to a game, she might have a heart attack.

It came time to play a team that beat them 56-0 the previous year. Coach Oakes gave a fiery pre-game speech. The first half, the teams hit, clawed and tackled each other to a draw. Deep into the third quarter, the game remained scoreless, a victory of sorts for Santa's underdogs.

Then the favorites scored. Santa's underdogs fumbled. The favorites scored again. Santa's underdogs fumbled again.

Frustrated, the next time the offense took the field, Coach Oakes told Santa, "The hell with it. You call the play." Santa called a sprint-out pass. At the snap, he rolled right and fired. The other team intercepted and scored again.

Coach benched his entire first string, including Santa. In a span of eight minutes, the other team had scored four touchdowns en route to a 27-0 victory.

Basketball season rolled around. The coach was George Hailey, a disciplinarian. Both he and Coach Oakes later would be enshrined in the Mississippi High School Coaches Hall of Fame.

Santa prayed he would avoid the cut and make the "B" team, known in some schools as the junior varsity. Coach Hailey kept only as many players as he had uniforms to offer. On cut day, the last uniform went to Santa.

When track season arrived, Santa decided to test his speed. He excelled at the quarter mile. Coach Oakes, who also coached track, insisted that Santa learn to run the hurdles, too. One evening, he set up a hurdle and talked Santa through the proper technique for leading with one leg and snapping the second leg down quickly after clearing the hurdle.

Santa blasted down the track, picking up speed. He stretched his lead leg forward but clipped the hurdle and fell, scraping his body along the packed dirt. Coach sent him back to do it again. Over and over Santa ran, until he cleared the hurdle cleanly several times. Then coach added a second hurdle. He and Santa worked until dusk. Before long, Santa became one of the top hurdlers in his conference.

Sometimes he also ran the mile relay. He tried the high jump but realized he wasn't any good at that.

Summer came and went. That fall, Santa again invested in football, which turned into an equalizer for him. It didn't matter that he was poor if he could play well.

Basketball remained a challenge. Again playing on the second team, Santa watched Cecil direct the varsity from point guard. Coach Hailey encouraged the 5-foot-10 Santa to keep practicing.

The summer before his senior year, Santa spent some time with his mother in Memphis while his grandmother visited Uncle J.W. in Alabama. Toward the end of summer, Santa boarded a Greyhound bus to pick up his grandmother. He took a seat next to a teenager named Cissy, who was headed to Florida to visit her father. They enjoyed a wonderful conversation. Santa asked for her name and address and promised to call her some time. "Okay," she said.

School started again. When basketball season arrived, Cecil shifted to sagging guard, where Coach Hailey liked to play his best shooter. Cecil could shoot from the floor almost as accurately as he could hit a free throw, and Cecil was one of the state's best free-throw shooters.

Santa took over as point guard, directing the varsity the way he'd watched Cecil do it the previous year.

Coach Hailey taught his players a diamond press, which could be sprung from any point on the court. Sometimes, they used it the full distance, other times from the three-quarter point or even mid-court. More than once, they pulled out a late victory with it.

The small-town team won game after game until it came time to play Tupelo, a much bigger school. Tupelo's players beat them up, scratching and clawing and out-hustling them for rebounds and loose balls. Coach Hailey thought his team would have won, if only the officials had called more fouls.

On the way home, his players spilled out their anger. Getting beat stung. About 10 miles outside of town, they begged Coach Hailey to let them out so they could walk back to school. He dropped them off, drove to the gym, turned on the lights and revved up the furnace. When the players arrived, they spent about 90 minutes practicing fundamentals.

In one tournament title game, Santa stepped to the foul line with seconds remaining and made the winning free throws. In the Northern Mississippi tournament, Cecil sunk 33 of 33 free throws. They won the conference championship and the district championship and advanced to the state tournament, where they met Tupelo in the quarterfinals. Once again, they lost.

Still, they won 34 games against five losses, three to Tupelo. The season had been magical. Most agreed that their tiny school had the second-best team in Mississippi.

That spring, Santa excelled again at track, especially the quarter mile, which he ran while wearing his favorite ball cap turned backward. It was his lucky cap. He couldn't lose as long as he wore it.

Someone stole the cap at the North Mississippi championships. He took second in the quarter mile and the high hurdles but still qualified for the state championships in Jackson. The week before the meet, his right calf swelled up, and Santa came down with a fever. The doctor said it was just a charley-horse, so Santa went to the meet hoping to run. His leg hurt so badly, he watched instead. He felt cheated, until he learned later his charley-horse really was a blood clot in a vein. Good thing he didn't run.

Santa's English teacher doubled as the school principal. He taught Santa how to write, how to think. He opened Santa's eyes beyond small-town Mississippi to a broader future. Santa dreamed big. Sometimes, though, he felt those dreams slipping away.

After graduating, he took a summer job at the saw mill making $44 a week. One day as he walked to the mill, the local district attorney drove past in his Mustang convertible and slowed.

"Where are you going this early?" he asked.

"The mill," Santa said.

"Would you like to work for me?"

"Yes, sir!" Santa exclaimed.

"Don't you want to know how much it pays?"

Santa didn't care. It would be better than the hot saw mill or the woods where they cut timber. He disliked the loud chain saws and the humid hollows where the breeze seldom swirled. He feared the cottonmouths and rattlesnakes. The mill itself was dangerous, too. Once, a worker's clothing got snagged in a conveyor belt, which pulled him across machinery and dropped him in hot coals left from burning bark.

Santa ran errands for the district attorney for $50 a week.

If he wanted to court a girlfriend, he double-dated or borrowed someone else's car. One weekend, the district attorney loaned him the green Mustang, with its black vinyl top and six-cylinder engine.

Santa cruised to the country to pick up his date, a girl from school. He arrived a little early, so he sat in the car with the top down in her driveway and let the breeze wash his face. Their kitchen window was open. He heard the girl and her mother arguing.

"I don't know what you see in him," the mother yelled. "He'll never amount to a hill of beans. He's nothing but white trash."

Stung by her words, Santa sat quietly for a long time, until he felt they had left the kitchen. He put the car in neutral and let it coast slowly back down the drive, then turned on the engine and pulled in again, as if he'd just arrived.

He continued to date that girl for a short time, but her mother's words haunted him long after they broke up. *He's nothing but white trash.* Was he?

Some day, he was going to own a new Cadillac. He just knew it.

Yet, deep down, he felt unsure of his future. In small-town Mississippi, there was little for young men to do but work at the mill, pick cotton or dig sweet potatoes. None of that would earn him a new Cadillac. Kids like him thought about marrying into money, but the reality was that well-to-do girls always ended up with the well-to-do guys. No, if he were to succeed, Santa would have to leave town.

He landed an athletic scholarship to play football at a junior college. An uncle drove him. Santa held back tears as he left grandmother, again.

During the ride, he remembered what his former girlfriend's mother had said about him being white trash. He didn't want her to be right.

He wanted to amount to more than "a hill of beans."

Five

Homeless in Houston

The young salesman awoke from a cold night's sleep inside his yellow Datsun four-door sedan.

Just 22 years old with some college behind him, Santa already had worked a number of door-to-door sales jobs. Every time, the bosses lured him with tales of easy money and quick sales. Sometimes, their tales turned true. While working for one company, he often had earned more in a week than many people earned in a month.

But something about each of the jobs eventually soured him. He disliked burdening customers — many of them poor — with overly high prices or slick, high-interest payment schemes. Dishonest sales pitches made him feel dirty.

He quit one job the first day because he didn't feel right about the opening line the company insisted he use at strangers' doors.

Now, on a blustery winter morning in 1971, he was stranded in Houston, Mississippi, the county seat of Chickasaw County. Out of money and out of luck, he'd slept eight nights in his car. He'd eaten only one meal in two days. Hungry and desperate, he had to do something.

He'd gotten in this mess because another sales job had gone bad. This time, he'd been pitching two products to families in and around Houston, which he was using as his home base. It was a small town, with a population of maybe 2,500, surrounded by farm land.

When he first arrived, Santa had set up a small office above a drug store on the square. He slept in a local motel. Without friends to keep him company or tempt him into slapping cues against balls in

41

a pool hall, he delved into his work. He toiled five and a half days a week, always taking off Sundays.

The man for whom Santa worked provided the start-up money and regularly mailed Santa his expense and pay checks through general delivery to the U.S. Post Office in Houston. The checks arrived each Thursday. Not one to save money, or worry about paying for things in the future, Santa lived paycheck to paycheck.

A few months into the job, his weekly paycheck check failed to arrive. Santa called the home office and got the receptionist.

"Everything's okay," she said. "No, I don't know why the check is late. It's on its way."

Days passed. No check arrived.

Santa called the office again and heard the same answer: Everything was fine. Don't worry. The money is coming.

After a few more days, he called again. This time, no one answered. The phone had been disconnected.

Santa's face flushed as he hung up the receiver.

He walked back to the motel and asked the clerk to let him stay. Santa already was a week overdue on his bill.

"Sorry," the clerk said, shaking his head.

Santa retreated to his car. That night, he made a pillow by stuffing a bag with clothes. Mississippi's winter air chilled him. He turned on the car's engine and ran the heater.

During the night, his gas tank emptied. The engine fluttered and stopped. A chill soon invaded the now-silent car.

The second night, Santa dressed in layers and huddled under the only blanket he owned. It was cheap and thin. He draped his coat over the blanket, which felt a little like grandmother adding an extra quilt, except the coat wasn't as big or warm.

On the sixth day, he ate the last meal he could pay for at midmorning. Then, though he still doubted a miracle, he hiked once again to the Post Office. Once again, no check had arrived.

The seventh day, swallowing his pride, he walked to a church to seek help. Unfortunately, the person who ran the assistance program for the poor was gone. Dejected, Santa turned away.

That day, he ate nothing.

After his eighth night in the car, Santa awoke hungry. He'd eaten only once in two days. He crawled out of the car and stretched.

He wore a green-and-black checked polyester coat. Grease spots marred his clip-on tie, the only tie he owned. He'd grown grubby and smelly.

Around the corner from Walgreens, a man Santa called Cookie ran a small brick-front cafe called the Dixie Diner. With a seating capacity of 27, the diner offered breakfast and lunch served at booths or along the counter, where customers sat on orange leather stools.

Cookie served as chief cook, cashier, custodian and dishwasher. Customers watched him grill their food behind the counter, flipping sizzling hamburgers or stirring grits. The comforting aroma of fresh-baked biscuits wafted through the air, mingling with the tang of fresh coffee. Many of the customers were regulars, including milk delivery drivers who arrived at 4:30 each morning, just as the diner opened.

Earlier in his stay in Houston, Santa had bought coffee and a couple of meals at the Dixie Diner. Now he headed back, brainstorming how he would eat without paying. Years earlier, he'd gotten out of trouble with Cecil by promising him a big bag of candy, which he never delivered. This predicament appeared more difficult to solve.

He selected a stool near the cash register and ordered a huge breakfast. Eggs, ham, biscuits, gravy. When it arrived, he gulped it down then sipped coffee refills while the breakfast crowd thinned. Finally, the time came to leave.

Santa patted his empty pocket. He jumped up and looked under his stool. He stepped outside and glanced at the sidewalk. He returned, looking worried.

"Oh, man, I lost my wallet," he said.

Cookie lifted a counter top door, walked out from behind the counter, looked around Santa's stool and bent down to pick up something.

"You must have dropped this," he said, handing Santa a twenty-dollar bill.

That was a lot of money, many times what his breakfast cost. It could more than fill a gas tank with gas selling at 19.9 cents per gallon. In fact, $20 was more than Cookie cleared some slow days in the diner.

Santa's heart pounded. He snatched the bill from Cookie's hand.

"Thanks, Cookie," Santa said, somewhat relieved but as nervous as a student who'd just cheated on a final exam.

Santa paid his bill, left a tip and dashed outside and around the block to his car. Adrenalin pumping, he put the car in neutral and pushed it to a gas station to fill up. He kept looking over his shoulder, worried that the person who lost that money would come looking for him. As soon as the pump shut off, he paid the attendant and drove off, eager to flee Houston as quickly as possible.

As he drove, his nerves slowly began to calm. He turned west, toward the Mississippi Delta. As he thought about the $20, guilt overcame him. Someone might have needed that money. He shouldn't have taken it. He should have admitted it wasn't his. He thought about Mrs. Barbee's pocketbook and how wrong it had been to take her money.

Trying to rationalize his good fortune and make himself feel better, he decided that Cookie had given him that money. Yeah, that was what happened. No one lost it. Somehow, Santa figured, Cookie knew he was in trouble and helped in a way that allowed Santa to maintain his dignity.

Cookie had saved him.

He offered a prayer of thanks and added: "Lord, if I'm ever in a position to help other people, that's what I'm going to do."

Six

Remembering a promise

A few months after he fled the Dixie Diner as a homeless salesman, Santa decided to leave the South in search of better opportunities.

He stopped in Memphis to say goodbye to his grandmother, who was staying with Santa's mother. Grandmother looked Santa in the eye, pinched his cheek between her thumb and forefinger and announced: "Honey, this is the last time I'm ever going to see you."

"Mama, get out of here!" he answered. "No it's not. I'm coming back."

Soon after that, Santa boarded a Greyhound bus to Kansas City.

It sounded like a good place for a fresh start. A big city by comparison to other places Santa had lived, its diverse economy somewhat insulated it from national recessions. Known for barbecue and jazz, it was Missouri's second-largest city and growing, along with its suburbs.

A year earlier, the Kansas City Chiefs had won Super Bowl IV. The Royals, a baseball expansion team, were building a strong foundation. And Kansas City soon would add professional basketball with the Kings.

Most important, though, was that Santa had a cousin in the Kansas City area who had encouraged him to head north.

Santa's bus pulled into the downtown station June 20, 1971. Carrying $18 in his pocket and one small brown suitcase, Santa disembarked amid strangers.

He stayed with his cousin until he found a sales job and rented a

Kansas City apartment. Eventually, he fell in love, married a local girl and moved to a suburb. Using her car as collateral, they borrowed money for a honeymoon at a Missouri lake resort.

A month later, he and his wife spent a pleasant Saturday with her parents at their farm. While they were gone, Santa's cousin drove out from Kansas City, knocked on Santa's door, peered in his windows and left.

A few days later, Santa called the cousin to chat.

"Where you been?" the cousin demanded.

"Right here," Santa answered, a bit perplexed.

"I tried to find you," the cousin said before blurting: "We buried grandma yesterday."

Santa's mouth dropped open.

"You what?" Anger turned his face red. He could barely talk. He didn't even know his grandmother had been ill or that she recently had moved to a Mississippi nursing home.

"I came and beat on your door," the cousin said.

"Why didn't you leave me a note?" Santa asked.

The cousin didn't answer. After they hung up minutes later, Santa called other relatives.

"How could you do such a thing?" he asked one.

"Why didn't you call," he asked another.

Each had an excuse. "We didn't have your phone number," one said. "We thought (your cousin) was going to tell you," answered another.

Santa's anger mixed with deep guilt and an empty sadness. He hadn't seen his grandmother in nearly two years, not since that day they said goodbye in Memphis. He figured she'd always be around. Instead, she had been right when she told him, "This is the last time I'm ever going to see you."

Early the next year, when a work assignment took Santa to Memphis, he drove the extra miles south to his hometown. Relatives had buried his grandmother next to his grandfather. A small bouquet of flowers sat on their graves. Santa drove to a local floral shop and bought more.

Returning, he knelt and placed his flowers. Then he wept.

§ § §

For years, money remained tight for Santa and his wife. They lived in a government-subsidized apartment. Santa talked his barber into cutting his hair on credit, with the understanding that Santa would pay when he could. Owners of a cafe let him run a tab, again with the understanding he would pay when he could. One day, unable to make his car payments, he lost the car to repossession. Realizing how much he needed a car, he scraped up money and got it back.

Blessed with an outgoing nature that made conversations with strangers easy, Santa seemed a natural to succeed in any sales job. His father-in-law saw so much potential, he put up his farm as collateral so Santa could get a $4,500 loan to start his own business. Santa opened an office on the Independence Square.

He sold the same item he had been pitching successfully for his previous employer, and at half the price. But he'd underestimated the value of an established company's name and credibility. Santa struggled. Two customers never paid their bills, leaving him unable to pay his office rent.

One day, needing enough money for milk, he scrounged up empty pop bottles for the deposit money. He'd never felt lower. He had let his wife and son down. He had let his father-in-law down, too.

On a November night, at wit's end, he decided to rob a small convenience store not far from his apartment. He borrowed a loaded .22-caliber revolver, stuck it under the front seat of his beat-up old Mustang, climbed in and turned the key. He backed across the snow-dusted lot and headed toward the street, his heart racing. Before getting far, he slammed his brakes and burst into tears.

Lord, what am I doing? he asked. *This is crazy! I've lost it. I can't do this.*

He turned the Mustang around and parked. In the deepening

SANTA'S SECRET: A STORY OF HOPE

cold, he briefly considered putting the revolver to his head.

You selfish SOB, he thought. *How could you possibly do that to your family?*

He sat in the car for a long time, praying. "God, I need your help. I'm in deep trouble. I'm a failure, but I need your help."

Eventually, he went inside. His wife sat on a couch in their small living room, reading a book near a lamp. They'd bought the couch at a garage sale. Santa couldn't think of anything to say, so he walked past her silently.

Five minutes later, the phone rang. It was one of Santa's brothers-in-law, a local postal carrier.

"Whatcha doing?" the brother-in-law asked.

"Oh, just sitting here."

"Can you come over to my house? I'd like to talk to you about something."

"What is it?"

"Just come on over. I don't want to talk about it over the phone."

Santa hung up and told his wife where he was going. When he arrived, his brother-in-law escorted him into a quiet room.

"You're in trouble, aren't you?" he said. It was more of a statement than a question. Santa looked away.

"Uh, what do you mean by trouble?"

"You are in trouble — financially."

"Well, it hasn't been good."

"Come clean. You are broke."

His brother-in-law offered to help, but Santa shook his head. "I don't need any help," he insisted. His brother-in-law pushed harder.

Suddenly, Santa realized that he had to accept. This was a miraculous answer to his prayers. Through Santa's brother-in-law, God was rescuing Santa.

"Thanks," Santa mumbled.

The men itemized Santa's debt and drew up a budget. Santa needed about $5,000 to pay bills for three months and afford groceries, they figured. His brother-in-law provided a loan.

That week, Santa found a job.

§ § §

Two weeks before Christmas 1978, a new boss told Santa: "You're fired." Santa soon found another job in a similar line of work and started over.

The next year, it happened again. Less than two weeks before Christmas, his boss told Santa he wouldn't be needed any more. This rocked Santa, who thought he had been doing a great job.

Days passed. Christmas neared.

Driving through Independence the afternoon of Christmas Eve, Santa heard his stomach growl. He pulled into a tiny drive-in burger joint, not much bigger than a one-stall garage. Santa ordered a hamburger and a Coke from a young carhop. When she returned with his food, Santa noticed her tiredness, discolored teeth and thin coat, which provided little protection against the bitter cold. She shivered.

She's not out here working just because she wants to be, Santa thought.

He took his food and handed her a twenty-dollar bill.

"I'll have to go inside to break this," the woman said.

At that moment, Santa decided she needed the change more than he did.

"Keep it," the out-of-work salesman told the downtrodden carhop.

Tears welled in her eyes.

"Sir, you have no idea what this means to me," she said, not realizing that he did, indeed, realize what it meant. She rushed back inside before her generous customer changed his mind.

Santa smiled. Despite being unemployed, he harbored no regrets. Giving her his change made him feel good. Suddenly, a memory flashed through his mind. He was at the Dixie Diner, homeless and hungry. Cookie gave him $20 when he couldn't pay for his breakfast. The emotions flooded back.

He closed his eyes.

Lord, I did make a promise to you, he prayed. *I don't have much, but...*

He opened his eyes and looked around. Backing away from his burger joint parking space, he pulled onto the street and headed for his bank. A little nervous and a little excited, he withdrew part of the $600 that remained in his checking account.

He headed to a government-funded housing complex. As he drove the streets looking for people to help, he felt uncomfortable. This didn't seem like a good place to approach strangers. He turned around and headed back toward the business district. He pulled into a service station lot, got out and handed a gift to a stunned clerk.

He circled a grocery store parking lot before driving to a small convenience store, where he parked and waited. A woman in a beat-up car pulled into the lot. Santa got out and handed her some money.

"Oh, thank you!" she exclaimed.

Their reactions warmed Santa. It felt as if he'd given himself a Christmas present just by helping others.

The new year arrived. Santa won his job back. After a few months, he landed a better job. By the end of 1980, his professional life had improved enough that he and his wife fled their apartment, bought a house and purchased a better vehicle.

He felt grateful. It was as if the Lord had told him: *Have you studied your lessons? If you do the right thing, I'll take care of you.*

Along came Christmas. Santa withdrew more cash and gave it away.

For Christmas 1981, he asked the teller for hundred-dollar bills, a denomination he's stuck with ever since.

From year to year, when possible, he increased the amount he withdrew. Ten thousand dollars. Twenty thousand dollars.

One day in Kansas City, after Santa handed out a few bills, a man demanded more. Santa shook his head, acted like it was all gone and ducked into his car. Maybe it wasn't a good idea to stand and chat, he decided. Maybe, too, it wasn't such a good idea to be carrying all this money alone.

He explained his problem to a friend named Kenneth, a former

Marine.

"Can you go with me?" Santa asked.

"Sure," Kenneth said.

One day, strangers chased them in a car. Santa and Kenneth escaped by running a red light.

"Wow!" Santa said. "I don't want to do that again."

Some friends in law enforcement suggested he get professional help. A Jackson County sheriff's deputy agreed to accompany Santa.

Meanwhile, as Santa refined his strategy, something happened in the downtrodden neighborhoods he often scoured. Stories spread about his Christmas appearances. Some people began watching for him, though many figured they'd never be so lucky as to see him.

Not knowing his name, they began calling him the "hundred-dollar-bill man."

Seven

Finding father

Santa suspected that his birth certificate contained a big fat lie. A man named Fred was listed as his father, but Fred never visited, never called and never wrote him — not when Santa lived with his grandparents, not during Santa's turbulent stay with his divorced mother in Memphis and not after Santa matured and started his own family.

Wouldn't a father care, at least a little?

Santa thought over the facts he did know. His mother had given birth to three children after marrying. Santa arrived first, followed by a boy 11 months later and a girl five years later. Not long after that, Santa's mother divorced her husband, who moved to Little Rock.

Santa's mother raised Santa's sister in Memphis. An uncle in Ohio took in Santa's brother.

The situation had puzzled Santa off and on for decades.

In the 1970s, Santa had tracked down a phone number for Fred in Arkansas. Santa picked up a phone in Missouri and called. Fred answered.

"Hi," Santa said before giving his name. There was a strained silence. Santa added, "I'm your son."

"Oh," Fred said. "Well, how have you been, boy?"

The tone of Fred's voice implied it had only been a short while since they last talked. Actually, they had never spoken. This made Santa uneasy, but he decided to push the conversation anyway.

They chatted for a half hour. Santa tried to get Fred to open up, but nothing worked. Santa even told Fred he'd begun using Fred's last name as a second middle name.

"Oh, that's nice," Fred said.

After hanging up, Santa turned to his wife and said, "Honey, that man is *not* my father."

Santa's grandmother never had revealed anything helpful about Santa's lineage. At one point, Santa nearly cajoled an uncle into spilling the beans, but the uncle held back. Before Santa got another chance to ask, the uncle died. Santa knew he should have pushed harder. He felt confident the uncle had wanted to tell him something.

When Santa's sister was growing up in Memphis, she and their "father" exchanged letters regularly. Once, while visiting his mother in Memphis, Santa ran across some of those letters. They didn't reveal much. Still, they made Santa wonder why Fred never contacted him.

By now, Santa's grown sister had moved to the Kansas City area, and they saw each other more often. As he and his sister talked one day in 1989, Santa brought up the topic of their brother, whom they barely knew. The brother didn't seem to want anything to do with them. Santa and his sister felt bad about this.

An idea popped into Santa's head.

"Let's just jump in an airplane and go see him," he insisted. "We'll walk up, say, 'Hi, it's us. We may never talk again, but this one time we'd just like to sit down and talk with you.' "

Both liked the idea, but they put it off. Santa decided maybe he should try to learn more about their brother and father first. But how?

Santa called Clarence Kelley, a former Kansas City police chief who'd been director of the Federal Bureau of Investigation from shortly after the Watergate scandal unfolded until shortly after President Jimmy Carter took office. Kelley had returned to Kansas City and established an investigation and security organization.

"Chief," Santa told him, "I need someone I can trust to check someone out."

"You'll get a call this afternoon," Kelley responded.

It came from one of Kelley's investigators, a man named Bill who recently had retired from the FBI. They talked. Santa laid out what he wanted to know. About a week later, Bill sprung expected but still-unsettling news on Santa.

"I don't think Fred is your father," Bill said.

As Bill sat in Santa's office, Santa picked up his phone and did something he should have done earlier. He dialed his mother. It was time for a well-rehearsed bluff.

"Mother," he said in a firm tone, "I know now that Fred is not my real father. Would you please tell me who my real father is? I'd like to know."

Silence.

Santa held his breath. So did his mother — until she caved.

"Charles Sullivan," she blurted. She feared that Santa would explode.

The news hit like a wall of bricks cascading on him. But Santa wanted to know more, and he needed to press while his mother was in a talking mood.

"Mother, you've been carrying this burden around for 40 years and it's off your shoulders now," he said, pausing to plan his next line of questioning. "Where does he live?"

"The last time I heard from him, he lived in Florida. I think he passed away just a few years ago."

Passed away?

Santa finally had the answer to his family's biggest secret — or at least, one of the biggest — and he still couldn't bring his life full circle. He craved to meet this man, to study his face and mannerisms, to ask him all kinds of questions, to learn about his life and hobbies and family. But that opportunity had been stolen from him, just as the chance to know his father while growing up had been taken away. This man — his honest-to-goodness real father — was dead.

Santa's heart sank.

He quizzed his mother a little more. She had been in the audience of a radio trivia game show in Memphis when she was called down front as a contestant. Charles Sullivan was the host.

They dated. She began to fall in love. She got pregnant. Before she told Charley about the baby, she picked up a newspaper in the restaurant where she worked and saw in the society section that Charles Sullivan was engaged to a local beauty queen. It tore her up. She resumed dating another man. She led him to believe the baby was his. They quickly married.

One month before Santa was born, she told her husband the truth. He booted her from their home. She had nowhere to go but to her parents in Mississippi.

That's how Santa ended up being raised by his grandparents.

Mom had another secret. She had another fling with Charley years later. He was the father of Santa's sister, too. It was a secret his mom never divulged to her husband.

Some pieces of his strange puzzle had come together, but Santa yearned to learn more. So he dispatched Bill the investigator to Memphis to research Charles Bonifay Sullivan.

Bill called one night from a Memphis hotel room with interesting news.

"I'm looking at a picture in a newspaper," Bill said, "and if it didn't have another name on it, I'd think it was you."

The picture, of course, was a black-and-white print of Charley Sullivan.

After Bill returned to Kansas City, he handed Santa a 31-page report that included interview notes, phone numbers of Sullivan's acquaintances, newspaper clippings, a marriage certificate and divorce records.

Also tucked inside was a photocopy of Charles B. Sullivan's 1985 obituary from *The Commercial Appeal* in Memphis.

Charley B. Sullivan, a Mid-South sportscaster and a pioneer in television in Memphis, died Tuesday in Pensacola, Fla., of an apparent heart attack. He was 63.

Services will be at 10 a.m. tomorrow at Harper-Morris Memorial Funeral Home in Pensacola with burial in Pensacola.

Sullivan, who began his broadcasting career at a Pensacola station in 1939, came to Memphis in 1940 as an announcer for WMC radio. His voice was the first on WMCT-TV (Channel 5) here in 1948.

He later changed from WMC and WMC-TV to WHBQ and WHBQ-TV (Channel 13), where he introduced a live studio wrestling show. But he was best known as the play-by-play voice of the Ole Miss Football Network for eight years...

Ole Miss? Santa gasped. He'd listened to Charley Sullivan call Ole Miss games on the radio. He'd listened to his father! What's more, he'd seen his father on television!

He looked at the obituary again, which went on for nine more paragraphs. It said Charley Sullivan called Ole Miss' first Sugar Bowl game in 1953 and later became station manager for WHER radio, which pioneered the telephone talk show in the mid-1960s. After Martin Luther King's assassination in 1968, he helped screen calls to the show. Later, he retired to Florida to care for his aging parents.

Santa stared at the last paragraph. *He leaves four daughters...*

Tears formed in Santa's eyes. He had four sisters — half-sisters, actually, — about whom he'd known nothing.

Santa read every page of Bill's report at least twice. His dad was a trivia show host. Santa once had his own local trivia game show on television. His dad loved sports, especially football. So did Santa. Both of them were athletic.

Heck, his dad participated in football, basketball, baseball and track in high school — exactly the same sports that acted as Santa's equalizer, making him more of a peer to his classmates, despite his poverty. His dad also played football and baseball in junior college. Santa had played football and baseball in junior college.

The divorce papers, filed by Charley's two wives, were a different story. They contained unkind words. Charley drank too much. Charley chased one wife and their children with a butcher knife. Charley blackened a wife's eye.

Santa winced.

Down a few paragraphs, two surprising words, barely visible within a faded paragraph, leaped out.

Your complainant would further show that the defendant has told her that he was going to leave his entire estate to his illegitimate son … The complainant knows nothing of this, but his references to this child are a source of humiliation and embarrassment to her.

Illegitimate son! Charles Sullivan knew he had a son!

Charley never willed anything to Santa. At least, not as far as Santa knew.

Santa pondered what he'd learned. Days passed.

Eventually, he got up enough nerve to call the first Mrs. Sullivan. His fingers shook as he punched her numbers. The phone rang. She answered.

"Hi," he said. "My name is …. I live in Kansas City. I hope you don't think I'm some kind of a quack. I'd be glad to give you my telephone number first."

"That's okay," she said. "How can I help you?"

Santa took a breath.

"I don't know how to say this, except that I think Charles Sullivan is my father."

He paused.

"I know," she said.

"Excuse me?"

"I know."

There it was. Confirmation. Santa had craved it. Now he craved more.

"I really apologize," he said slowly, "but how do you know?"

"Charley and I used to have some really bad fights," she said. "Charley would get drunk. Charley was not a real pleasant person to be around when he was drinking. One night, we got into a big fight and he told me. It was 1961."

"Wow," Santa said.

"He told me he had a son, how old you were, where you were born. I never really believed it, but I wrote it down in my journal anyway. I just thought Charley was telling me something to be mean to me."

There it was. Just like her divorce petition said. Drinking. Arguing. Talk of a son.

Santa asked permission to talk to her daughters. She said that would be okay, but she wanted to call them first and let them know.

The eldest was named Elizabeth. Santa started with her.

He dialed. About five minutes into their conversation, she interrupted Santa with an unexpected question.

"Do you remember a long time ago being on a bus?"

He thought for a minute. A light went on.

"Oh my goodness," he said. He suddenly recalled an address of a girl he'd been smitten by during a 1965 bus ride from Memphis to Alabama. "900 Brower," he spouted.

"Oh my God!" she exclaimed. "It is you!"

"Cissy Sullivan?" he asked.

"Yes," she said, confirming her nickname.

His mouth fell open.

This was the girl he'd met on the bus the summer before his senior year in high school, when he left Memphis to pick up grandmother in Alabama. Cissy had been on her way to visit her father in Pensacola. The next year, when Santa visited Memphis, he called her several times for a date but she always had an excuse. Later, he learned she was younger than he thought, so he stopped his pursuit.

Now Cissy told him something new. When she arrived at the Pensacola bus station, her dad picked her up. They started for his home.

"How was your trip?" he asked.

"I met this nice boy from Mississippi," she reported.

"Oh, really? Where is he from?"

She told him Santa's hometown. He asked the boy's name. She told him. Charley Sullivan punched the brakes, pulled the car onto the shoulder and turned to look his daughter. He asked question after question, studying her face.

"Dad," she said, "why do you want to know so much about him?"

He turned away and looked at the road.

"I think I know the kid's father," he answered, dropping the subject.

After Cissy finished her story, Santa smiled. It sure was a small world.

Even after contacting his new-found sisters, something still nagged Santa. He needed to go to Pensacola.

During a trip to Florida, he stopped at the graveyard where Charles Sullivan lay buried. He found the gravestone. Sullivan's parents were buried there, too.

Santa stopped to talk to the caretaker. He explained why he was there.

"Son," the caretaker said, "your dad was out here about every day. That man lived out here. He had a chair and a parasol. He'd come out here and bring a book. He'd sit there and talk to his mom and dad, just like they were there. He'd stay out here sometimes all day. One day, I was making my rounds, I looked up there, and Mr. Charley was draped over his mother's grave. He dropped dead right there."

Santa had a feeling his father died a very lonely man with a broken heart.

Eight

A childhood debt

After flying south for his 20-year high school reunion, Santa drove to his Mississippi hometown and stopped at a store. He walked inside.

"Hi," he said to a clerk.

"What can I get you today?" the clerk asked.

Santa pointed. "Give me some of those. I'll take some of those, too. They look good."

The clerk filled two large brown paper sacks with a variety of goodies, rang up the tab and handed the bulging bags to Santa.

That evening, Santa sneaked the bags into the community center and hid them.

Their class had graduated 72 seniors. Not all made it back for this reunion, but a sizeable crowd formed as more and more husbands and wives walked into the building, smiling at the sight of old pals and friends. They shared hand shakes, hugs and a few pats on the back. Chatter and laughter splashed across the room. Some of their old teachers shared stories as well.

After dinner, classmates took turns standing and reminiscing. Santa let the evening unfold until he felt the time was right. Then he dug out the two brown bags and stood.

"I have a debt I want to pay off," he announced.

Seated one table away, Cecil turned to look at his old friend. Cecil, who knew Santa better than anyone with the possible exception of Santa's wife, wondered what trick or joke his jovial friend planned to unleash this time.

"I promised something," Santa began, "to a guy back in first grade."

Uh oh, thought Cecil. Suddenly, he knew where this was going.

Santa explained about the day he picked up a hickory nut on the playground and threw it, hitting a classmate in the eye. The classmate threatened to tell the teacher. Santa talked him out of it by promising him a big bag of candy. Day after day, the classmate asked for this candy. Day after day, Santa said he forgot.

"I never did pay him off," Santa admitted as he reached for the bags. "But tonight, I'm going to pay that debt off — with interest."

He handed Cecil the bags. Looking inside, Cecil figured the bill must have topped $75 or $100. He laughed.

"It's about time, you paying this off after 30-some years," Cecil said, "because I was getting ready to tell teacher on you."

Nine

'Santa *incarnate*'

An unusual offer over the telephone caught Santa by surprise. "Are you willing to appear on Oprah Winfrey's show?" the caller from Chicago asked.

Like Santa, Oprah grew up poor in Mississippi, earned success and enjoyed giving back by helping others. Santa thought the world of Oprah.

Appear on her show? A lump formed in his throat. How could he be interviewed on national television without someone recognizing him? He feared that if his identity were revealed, he wouldn't be able to spread Christmas cheer as Secret Santa anymore. It wouldn't be safe, for one thing. Knowing that Santa carried lots of money, some people would be tempted to rob him. If his name got out, people would come to his home and his business demanding money. They might go after his wife or his children.

Besides, he didn't give away money to gain recognition. He did it to fulfill a promise he'd made 24 years earlier, in 1971.

Was the thrill of meeting Oprah worth the risk of being revealed?

After pondering the situation, Santa decided a disguise might allow him to take part while still protecting his identity. He owned a fake white beard and mop of matching fake hair. They could hide much of his face.

Oprah's producer agreed to give Santa editorial control, meaning he could approve what Oprah planned to say about him. The producer also offered to pay Santa's airfare, but Santa declined. He felt uncomfortable providing his name to strangers, even if they worked for Oprah.

Santa recruited two of his children to accompany him. They flew to Chicago early one morning. A limousine picked them and other guests up from a hotel and took them to the studio where several shows would be taped that day, all to air later.

Excited chatter cascaded through the limousine. Some of the strangers began introducing themselves and their topics.

"Who are you?" someone asked Santa. Not yet in disguise, he hemmed and hawed a bit and changed the subject.

At the studio, Santa's children took seats in the audience. Santa slipped on a heavy Chiefs jacket and put on his fake hair, beard and mustache. The mustache was so thick and long, it concealed Santa's lips. When he talked, not even his mouth showed. He checked his disguise in a mirror, stroked a few loose hairs into place and took a deep breath. Well, he had promised to do it, and now it was time.

He walked onto the brightly lit stage and settled into a chair facing the studio audience. A clean-cut man in a gray suit, tie and white dress shirt took a seat to Santa's left.

Oprah entered wearing a white pant suit. She seated herself on the edge of the raised stage, practically in the audience's lap.

Looking into the camera, Oprah offered a tease:

"Coming up, if you are feeling down, if you need to rejuvenate your Christmas spirit, wait until you hear the story of this Secret Santa, who's really discovered the joy of giving. He gave away $40,000 to complete strangers last Christmas."

The image faded to black for a commercial break. When the camera came back on, Oprah looked into the lens.

"We all know Christmas is really about the joy of giving, but what would you do if a complete stranger just walked up to you on the street and gave you several hundred-dollar bills?"

She turned to the audience.

"What would you do?"

"Spend it," one woman answered. The camera zoomed in on her.

"Spend it?" Oprah asked. "Okay. Would you try to give it back?"

"I would wonder what he wanted," the woman said.

"Even if he looked like Santa?" Oprah asked.

"*Especially* if he looked like Santa," the woman said.

Many in the audience laughed. Oprah chuckled, too.

"Well," Oprah said, "my next guest is a Secret Santa who gave away $40,000 in cash last Christmas. Here's what his hidden Santa camera captured on tape."

Footage from the previous year, taped by a St. Joseph television station, appeared on television monitors. The clip opened inside a car. Though unseen, Santa sat near the camera and narrated.

"A lot of people need a lot of help," he said. "It's something I thoroughly enjoy doing. I have a great deal of fun."

The camera cut to two women and a man in a parking lot. Santa walked toward them as the camera followed.

"This is for you," Santa said, handing over a hundred-dollar bill. "Merry Christmas."

"For heaven's sake," one recipient said. "My gosh, Santa Claus. Oh, thank you."

As Santa turned away, the recipient asked: "Who is he?"

Then Santa gave more money to more strangers.

"You find somebody whose spirits might be a little low," he explained on the tape. "If you can just have a small impact on raising their spirit, giving them a little hope — that's why I do it."

Approaching two men, Santa handed each a Ben Franklin and announced: "I live in the South Pole. Way south. Merry Christmas."

As the men grinned, the tape faded to black. Oprah's audience applauded.

"Our Secret Santa lives in the Missouri area where he is a successful businessman," Oprah said, "but he grew up poor in Mississippi. So to maintain his secret identity, he is in disguise. He vowed as a young boy that he would give to people in need if he ever made it big."

She turned to Santa.

"So, how did you get started?"

In a nervous voice, Santa told his Christmas Eve 1979 story about stopping at a drive-up burger joint on a bitterly cold day and feeling sorry for the young lady who came out to take his order.

"I gave her a large bill, and she said, 'I'll have to go inside to change this.' I said, nah, just keep the change. She said, 'You're kidding.'"

Whether worried about his disguise or nervous about being on Oprah's show, Santa rushed his story. Words tumbled from his mouth. He forgot to breathe. He hadn't felt this nervous since giving his first speech in college.

"I drove away," he said, "and I never forgot the look on her face. So I thought, well, I'll do this a little more. I went and got a little money out of the bank ... I didn't start with hundred-dollar bills. As business got better, I began to give a little more."

"What did you start with?"

"I think it was a fifty," he blurted, though he meant to say a twenty.

After a short exchange, Oprah asked: "Since then you've given away how much? Do you keep track of it?"

A cat-and-mouse game began. Oprah really wanted an answer.

"I know, but I'd rather not say," Santa said. "It's — a lot."

"Oh, come on. Tell me."

"Nah, I can't."

"Like, uh," she started.

"I guarantee I don't get a tax deduction for it," he said.

"Yeah," Oprah said. She paused. Her voice grew stern: "Tell me." Santa hesitated.

"Last year I gave away forty grand," he said.

The audience applauded. Oprah asked Santa how he selected people to help. Santa explained how he drives through town, usually accompanied by law enforcement officers, and scours the streets for people who look needy.

"You just know the look, particularly if you've been there," he said. "I've been there. I know what it's like to live in a government project. I know what it's like to be poor."

He hesitated and brushed a piece of his fake beard away from his mouth.

"I know what it's like to have a beard in my mouth," he continued, drawing a laugh from Oprah. "But I've lived in the projects, and I understand what it means to have your utilities cut off, things like that. You can spot those people, particularly on a day when everybody else is working and they're out, especially when they've got that lost look, you know. It's so much fun. Giving this way allows people to maintain their dignity. They didn't apply for it, they didn't ask for it, they didn't have to stand in line. I admit I love doing it."

"I do too," Oprah said. "I remember driving along one day with my makeup artist and we saw this guy looking in trash cans, as people do, in the morning for food... Before he got to the next trash can, we filled the trash can with, like, bills so when he got to the next trash can, there would be all this money underneath all this trash, and he would, like, wonder.... So we rolled up the street and he got to it, and he was like — "

Oprah widened her eyes extra wide, grinned extra big and paused to let her audience see her expression. The audience roared. Oprah held the look for a second or two then relaxed her face.

"We should have had a camera," she said.

Her story reminded Santa of one of his own. He told about driving down an alley and seeing a man, woman and young child crawl out of a trash bin.

"They were sleeping in there," Santa said. "So we gave them $700 or $800."

He paused.

"I can tell you one thing. You get to witness every emotion, from suspicion, like the lady talked about, to disbelief, shock. You get the tears. But you get a genuine 'Thank you.' And that's why I do it."

Oprah cocked her head and announced: "Why, you are Santa *incarnate* right here."

Santa laughed softly.

Ready to introduce her next guest, Oprah launched into another rehearsed line.

"Most people don't have $40,000 to give away," she said, "but you don't have to have money to experience the joy of giving. Detective Mike Jones is a police officer in Panama City, Florida. He's known as Salvage Santa because he devotes his spare time to refurbishing toys for children."

She turned to Mike, the man in the gray suit next to Santa.

"You get a kick out of that?" Oprah asked.

"Yes ma'am."

"Yeah," Oprah said. She hesitated and shot Mike one of her looks. "Don't call me ma'am," she said. "I know your momma raised you right, but don't call me ma'am."

The audience roared again.

Oprah asked Mike his story. He explained that 12 years earlier, while working as an off-duty security officer for Sears & Roebuck, he saw workers crushing damaged toys in a back room. "Hold the machine, don't crush any more toys," he told them before scurrying off to ask someone in management for the damaged toys.

"I figured if I could get four or five of the same toy, I could fix two or three," he said. "Working 14 years as a detective in child abuse cases, I've seen a lot of children that don't have anything and that are taken out of homes. I thought I could get those gifts to them. From there it's been a steamroll."

Donors leave broken bicycles in his yard, and he fixes them, he said. The local media nicknamed him Salvage Santa because he's like a junkyard Santa Claus.

"We take junk toys," he said. "We repaint them, we rebuild them."

His goal, he said, was to fix 100 bicycles a year. The Fraternal Order of Police and a mom-and-pop drug store help by furnishing coloring books, crayons and other small items for Christmas stockings.

"But the citizens of Panama City, they make Salvage Santa what it is," he said. "I just fix the toys."

"When do you have time?" Oprah asked. "You're still a detective then?"

"Yes ma'am."

After another brief exchange, Oprah wrapped up for a break. Music played in the background as the show faded to a commercial.

Still in his chair on stage, Secret Santa decided to give Salvage Santa all the hundred-dollar bills he had left in his pocket. Mike had a flight to catch quickly and wouldn't be staying long enough for Santa to corral him after the show, so Santa reached in his pocket and pulled out the wad of bills. He leaned close to Mike, not expecting Oprah to be watching.

"Here you go," he whispered. "Here's a little something to help you out, Salvage."

Oprah's eyes moistened. She asked to see the money.

As the camera rolled again, it caught her talking to the men.

"Don't you cry because I will cry," she said. "That is the nicest thing that ever happened during the commercial break, I will say."

"Really?" someone in the audience asked.

Realizing the cameras were rolling again, Oprah explained.

"Hi everybody," she said. "During the commercial break, this is what happened. Secret Santa turned to Salvage Santa and said, 'Here, take this.' And this was, like, $1,600!"

Oprah showed the camera the bills and handed them back to Salvage Santa.

"And that's not all that happened during the commercial break," she continued. "This lady over here said, 'Hey, could we pass the hat?' I said, 'Pass the hat for what?' She said, 'Pass the hat for the kids.' I said, 'We never passed no hat before, but if you want to pass one, here it is.' "

She paused.

"That's the nicest thing to ever happen during a commercial break. Thanks."

Once again, the show faded to a commercial, this time with the camera following a red hat being passed through the audience. When the show resumed, Oprah explained that she didn't ask anyone to do this. It just happened.

Salvage Santa and his wife stood near her, holding two hats stuffed with about $400 in audience donations. He uses cash to buy bike parts or other items to fix toys.

"This is what our audience did," Oprah said to the camera. "Aren't they the nicest?"

"It's all about the act of giving," Salvage Santa said.

Oprah looked at the two Santas.

"Secret Santa, our audience: It's just like that random act of kindness. When you started it, everybody else got into it. I love my audience so much. This would not happen on another talk show. Thank you so much."

After the show aired, Santa returned to St. Joseph to hand out more cash. Wearing the same disguise, he walked into a coin-operated laundry. A lady sitting in a chair looked up.

"I know you," she said. "You were on 'Oprah.' "

That drew a laugh from Mike Strong, the commander of the Buchanan County Drug Strike Force, who accompanied Santa.

"Well Santa," he said, "I guess you'll have to stop wearing your disguise. People are starting to recognize you."

Santa laughed, too.

Later, he ditched the disguise.

Ten

'There *is* a Santa Claus'

Cars began pulling into Santa's driveway about 8:30 a.m. on a Friday, three days before Christmas 1995. His wife set juice, breakfast treats and napkins on the kitchen island.

Several elves, a security officer and a reporter and photographer were to rendezvous at Santa's house before he spread Christmas cheer through Kansas City and its suburbs of Belton, Grandview and Independence.

The previous day, he'd given away $12,000 in St. Joseph, about 50 miles to the northwest. Tipped by a law enforcement officer, Santa had visited a single mother raising 12 children. He arrived at her house wearing a Santa hat and announced, "Merry Christmas."

Several glum children stared back at him. Santa hesitated slightly before trying to draw them out of their shells.

"If someone will tell me Merry Christmas," he said slowly, "I'll give him a hundred dollars."

A few seconds passed.

"Merry Christmas, Santa," one child finally said.

Soon, the others greeted Santa, too. He handed out $3,000 — most of it to the mother — wished them all well and left.

A St. Joseph journalist following Santa stayed behind briefly. The mother explained that only five minutes before the strangers arrived, she pulled seven of her children together and explained that she couldn't afford Christmas. She hadn't even bought a tree.

Now, because of some anonymous Santa, Christmas would be Christmas again.

"I've always believed in guardian angels," the mother said, choking back tears.

Back in Jackson County the next morning, Santa had another special visit planned, one that included an unusual assist from a Blue Springs businessman. First, though, Santa had to finish getting organized.

His doorbell rang. A reporter for *The Kansas City Star* introduced herself. Santa had allowed Star reporters to follow him in previous years, but this reporter was new to his escapades. After a brief greeting, Santa sat with her at the kitchen table to explain his ground rules. He didn't want his face or even the back of his head or hair visible in any pictures, but it was okay to photograph his arms and hands. He didn't want his name or occupation revealed. He didn't do this for any recognition, he said.

His plans started with the special stop, after which he would zigzag through downtrodden neighborhoods. He'd hand out money swiftly and depart before anyone got wise and chased him.

That's where the reporters and photographers came in, he explained. He began inviting them to accompany him because he always wondered how recipients reacted to his gifts. He couldn't stay long enough to see for himself, because word spread quickly when he handed out money, and he didn't want to be surrounded by a mob.

The reporter nodded and asked why he gave away money in such a way.

Santa smiled and gave some of the same answers he told Oprah. He added: "This is my own Christmas present. It's probably against the law to have this much fun, to see their faces."

The doorbell rang again. A *Star* photographer entered, grinned at a giant Santa Claus standing in the foyer and playfully said, "Why, hello there."

As the photographer unbuttoned his coat and sat, Santa looked at his watch.

"Wait a minute," he said. "Where are the radios?"

He disappeared into his office and returned with hand-held

two-way radios. He plopped in fresh batteries, turned them on and fiddled with the frequency settings.

"These are new," he said, peering at the LCD screen over the top of his glasses. "I hope they work."

He handed one to the reporter and one to Sheriff's Department Captain Tom Phillips, who had provided security for Santa for a few years and was in the process of rising through the department's ranks. Though Tom hadn't known what to expect the first year, he became hooked after watching Santa pay $100 for coffee at a Sonic. The carhop screamed in delight and dashed back to the kitchen jumping the whole way.

Tom sometimes drove for Santa and sometimes rode shotgun, helping look for possible recipients and possible danger. More than once, he warned Santa away from potential "targets" if he felt something bad might happen.

Three elves soon arrived, including an Olathe, Kansas, man who had received a heart and lung transplant four years earlier. Santa had donated toward the surgery's expense, but he'd never met the man until now. They shook hands, grinning.

It was time to go. Santa and his elves climbed into a van Santa had rented to keep anyone from tracking him through the license plates. The reporter and photographer got into a nearby car and tested the radios.

They headed south to Belton, where a 71-year-old woman shared a small house with her daughter. In a letter that had been forwarded to Santa, the daughter had pleaded for help.

I have a request that is probably very unusual, and hard for me to ask, her letter began. *Quite simply, I am desperate and this is the only way I can think of to reach someone who might help us.*

She explained that her mother was legally blind, used a wheelchair and needed kidney dialysis three times a week. *Is there a reputable car dealer out there somewhere who would be willing to work with her on the purchase of a good, used DEPENDABLE minivan?*

Her mother's six-year-old car was "a rolling piece of junk," she said, and likely to give out on them at any time. They didn't have much, but by pooling their money they could afford payments of $100 to $150 a month. They needed a van because at some point, they would need a wheelchair lift for her mother to get in and out of the vehicle. *Please, is there anyone out there who will or can help us?* She signed her name and provided an address and phone number.

Santa had called Bob Balderston at Blue Springs Ford and talked him into splitting the cost of a used van. Then he called the woman, pretending to be someone who could check out car dealers for her. He said he'd need to stop by and ask a few more questions. They set an appointment to meet at her house and talk more.

Employees from Blue Springs Ford drove the van to her neighborhood and parked down the block until Santa and his elves arrived. Santa knocked, went inside and spoke briefly to the woman and her mother. Then he suggested they both look out the picture window.

As they did, a tan van with a giant scarlet ribbon tied on top pulled into their driveway. The daughter raced outside and trotted down a snow-covered wheelchair ramp screaming: "Oh my God! Oh my God!" She clasped her cheeks then clasped her hands as she stared in disbelief. Racing back in the house, she returned with her mother in the wheelchair.

Though gently used, the van looked new. Both women stared, their mouths open. Someone opened the passenger door. A large basket of Christmas food, including a frozen turkey, sat in the seat, courtesy of Blue Springs Ford employees.

Santa reached into a pocket.

"You say you owe about $700 on the Taurus?" he asked, unfurling a wad of money. He counted out $1,000 — the debt plus a little extra.

"There is a Santa Claus," the mother in the wheelchair exclaimed.

"No," answered her daughter, who was unable to take her eyes off the van. "There is a God in heaven."

Santa thanked the Blue Springs Ford employees who helped with the surprise then climbed into his van with the elves. Within minutes, his group pulled into the lot of a King Super Store. Santa handed the former transplant patient $100 before they entered. The man grinned. He selected a pack of gum for 27 cents, slipped the manager at the checkout counter the $100 and told her, "Keep the change."

The manager looked at the bill, looked at the man leaving and said, "Is he crazy? Or did he just win the lottery?"

Santa chuckled then gave each remaining employee a hundred-dollar bill of her own before swiftly leaving.

One ran outside after him waving her arms to get his attention.

"I want to thank you very much," she yelled as light snow swirled from a gray sky. "You don't know what this means to me."

The reporter followed her back inside, curious what she meant. Tears poured down the woman's face for several minutes. Every time she tried to speak, tears spouted again. She wiped her eyes, paused and wiped again.

"My husband is disabled, and I have kids," she finally said. "I can really use this."

Outside, the reporter and photographer saw that Santa's van was gone. They called on the radio.

"Look across the street," Captain Tom answered. "See the woman by the bus stop? Santa just gave her $100."

That woman also had burst into tears and was crying so hard that her body shook. Santa and Captain Tom circled around, returned and gave the woman $200 more. She sobbed some more.

And so the day went. A hundred dollars to every person in a coin-operated laundry, a hundred apiece to three persons walking through a trailer park, a hundred each to seven women inside Charlene's Hair Fashions in south Kansas City.

"Are you sure they are real?" one woman asked as she and others studied the bills in the hair salon.

"Read the serial numbers," Santa answered. "They're all different."

"I've never had anything given to me like this," one woman said. "I want to frame it, but I need the money. I'll never get over it. Who is this guy? I want to thank him."

The waitress at lunch received a $100 tip. A family with three small children received $400. Santa used two hundred-dollar bills for two cups of coffee at Sonic.

The capper came at an Independence pawn shop, where Santa spotted a couple lugging their color television inside. As the couple solemnly watched a clerk test the reception, Santa stepped behind them. He forced three crisp bills into the man's right hand, said "Merry Christmas from Secret Santa" and dashed out the door.

Stunned, the man sifted the bills between his fingers and thumb. Yes, the cash was real. His mouth dropped.

He glanced out the door, but the benefactor had vanished.

"I don't believe this," he said, realizing they could keep the television *and* buy gifts for their two children. "This is really happening? He just made my day."

Eleven

Fulfilling Mike's dream

Coach Hailey's son, Mike, needed a kidney.

Thirty years earlier, Coach Hailey had guided Santa's high school basketball team to a 34-5 record and the state semifinals during Santa's senior year. Mike, a 6-foot-5 sophomore on that team, had been the first sub off the bench, a fighter under the basket who could play forward or center equally well.

Now, diabetes had ruined Mike's kidneys. His name was on a waiting list for a kidney transplant. In the meantime, he endured dialysis. His skin tone yellowed. His energy waned.

When Santa heard about Mike's condition, his mind raced back to that wonderful season, when he and Cecil and the others won so many games. Thirty years had flown past. It would be great to see everyone again.

Santa organized a team reunion in Memphis. Nearly everyone came, including Coach Hailey and Mike and Cecil. They reminisced and laughed about the good old days before Santa took them outside for a surprise. Limousines waited. Santa wouldn't say where they were headed. The men climbed inside and watched as Tennessee vanished. Miles and miles of Mississippi landscape flashed past outside their windows. Eventually, the terrain grew exceedingly familiar. They were headed to the town where they had trained, played and matured together.

They arrived on the town square, climbed from the fancy cars and chatted like schoolboys. After awhile, Santa noticed that Mike had moved off by himself, near a car where he stared into space. Santa walked over to talk. Mike's eyes looked sunken, with dark patches under each.

"What's wrong?" Santa asked.

"I'm going to die," Mike answered.

Mike explained that he was on a transplant list but he didn't believe he would get a kidney. If not, he'd never do some of the things he'd dreamed about doing.

"Like what?" Santa asked.

"I always wanted to get a Harley-Davidson Fat Boy and ride through the country on it," Mike said.

They talked more about Mike's kidneys before Santa asked Mike if he could say a prayer for him. After he finished, Santa looked at Mike.

"You're going to get your kidney," Santa said. "And when you get better, I'll make your dream come true."

Mike's eyes grew wide.

"How are you going to do that?" he asked.

"Mike, you know me. I'll do it."

They rejoined the rest of the basketball team. Santa had bought new basketballs. The teammates headed for the school gym, where they shot free throws with the new balls and then autographed them. Each man got to keep a ball.

A few days later, Coach Hailey wrote to thank Santa for instigating such a wonderful weekend, perhaps the best of his life. *I could thank you a million times and it wouldn't be enough. I thought I was good at making plans work, but you have beat me by a mile…. My love for you and the other members of the 1966 team is forever.*

Months later, Mike's mother gave him one of her kidneys. Their surgeries in Birmingham went well. After Mike returned home, Santa called.

"I found a Fat Boy," Santa reported. "It's a little beat up and needs some work."

Mike didn't care if the used bike was a tad beat up. "I know someone who can fix it," he gushed.

"Okay," Santa said, grinning back home in Missouri as he pictured Mike's face. "I'll ship it to you."

When the truck arrived, it was too big for Coach's driveway, so the delivery men parked along a two-lane highway, about 100 yards from the house. When Mike saw the truck, he walked toward the highway to see what was inside. The delivery men opened the back and rolled out a fresh-off-the-showroom-floor Fat Boy. Its teal custom-paint job glistened.

Santa had teased Mike about it being a beat-up old bike. Instead, Santa had visited a Harley dealer in Kansas City and picked out a new one costing more than $20,000. Santa forewarned Coach Hailey and asked him to call when the motorcycle arrived so he could hear Mike's reaction.

Mike whooped and hollered.

Not well enough to take the bike for a spin that day, Mike parked it and waited. Weeks passed. Finally, he climbed aboard and disappeared down the road. Many months later, he and a friend hauled the motorcycle and a second one to Colorado, where they toured the state.

Mike was living his dream.

SANTA'S SECRET: A STORY OF HOPE

Twelve

The microwave lady

S anta dialed an old buddy's phone number.

"Hey, Cecil," he said. "Santa's coming to Mississippi. You want to go with me on the trip?"

Santa planned to visit Jackson, the state capital, and teach a wealthy business owner how to become a Secret Santa. He'd contacted the man, sent him newspaper articles and offered to show him how to find targets. The man had said yes.

If this went well, Santa planned to train more Secret Santas the next year, in 1999.

So, did Cecil want to join them?

"Sure," said Cecil, who'd never accompanied Santa on one of his giveaways. "That sounds like fun."

Weeks later, Cecil and Santa met at the airport in Memphis. Santa opened a bag and let Cecil peak inside. It contained two pairs of cheap sunglasses, two sets of fake hillbilly teeth and two ugly ball caps, each with long hair flowing from inside the caps. In these get-ups, no one would recognize them. And no one likely would want to get close, either.

Santa rented a white Lincoln. They climbed inside for a long ride south to Jackson. Along the way, they stopped in the town where they grew up. They parked in a service station lot, slipped on their disguises, laughed at each other and looked out the car's windows. A man with whom they'd played little league baseball walked past and stared. They stared back, unsmiling. After he passed, they cracked up.

"Did you see the look on his face?" Cecil said.

"Yeah," Santa said. "That was great."

Obviously, he didn't realize who they were. Perfect.

Santa drove to the Piggly Wiggly grocery store, where they spotted a young woman in the parking lot. Santa handed her a hundred-dollar bill.

"Praise the Lord!" she declared. "Thank you, thank you."

They headed to the town square and circled twice. Santa noticed a teenager who had the hood raised on his pick-up truck and was tinkering in the engine compartment.

"Let's get this guy," Santa said.

Santa pulled alongside and asked the young man what was wrong.

"I'm having trouble with my engine," he said.

Santa handed him a bill or two. The man's eyes widened. He didn't know what to say, especially to two ugly hillbillies in a beautiful white car.

Santa and Cecil pulled away and headed for the high school. Within minutes, Santa noticed in his rear-view mirror that a caravan of trucks had formed behind them. Apparently, the teenager on the square had a citizens band radio in his truck and had notified his friends about men in a white Lincoln handing out money.

"Uh, oh," Santa said, realizing that he couldn't stop now.

He glanced around. There weren't many places to hide or escape. He veered onto a different street and turned south. With the trucks tailing him, he headed toward the railroad tracks, crossed over and wove through the part of town where only African Americans lived. He was hoping that his posse didn't know this area well. Santa spun through streets and alleys, got ahead of the trucks, turned a corner and peeled onto a two-lane highway. Down the road, Santa and Cecil finally relaxed. The road behind them was empty. They took off their disguises. They were safe.

After arriving in Jackson later that day, they checked into a hotel and talked about plans for the next morning. The thought of training another Santa excited Secret Santa.

In the morning, the man's executive assistant called Santa at the hotel. The executive had to go to Washington, D.C., unexpectedly.

He couldn't accompany them.

"Shoot!" Santa said.

He looked at his good friend and smiled. At least they could still have some fun. They didn't need their disguises, either. No one in Jackson would know them. Two Jackson police officers, a retired FBI agent and the owner of a local security company had joined them, so they didn't have to worry about being chased either.

They got in the car. Santa wound through Jackson, looking for the downtrodden and telling Cecil how to find them. Eventually, they sauntered into a busy pawn shop. Wearing his usual white overalls and red shirt, Santa pretended to browse as he sized up the crowd.

Cecil noticed a cheaply dressed young woman with ruffled, unwashed hair. She carried a small microwave oven pock-marked with dents. Cecil wouldn't have paid a dime for it. But then, he didn't have to pay. As the woman waited behind a line of other customers, Cecil approached from one side.

"What are you doing?" he asked, speaking slightly above a whisper.

"I want to sell my microwave to get some money for Christmas," the woman said. Out of work, she needed money to buy gifts for her children.

"How much do you want?" Cecil asked.

"Whatever the guy will give me."

Santa saw Cecil talking to the woman and approached from the other side. Cecil looked at the microwave again and figured the woman would be lucky to get $20.

"I tell you what," he said. "I'll give you $100 for it."

The woman's brow furrowed. She looked at Cecil and cocked her head. Was this guy for real? There was a way to find out. She started to hand Cecil the microwave.

"I'll give you $200," Santa said.

The woman turned to her left and looked at Santa. Two crazy men in the same pawn shop? How could this be?

"No mister," Cecil said. "Not so quick. I was here first."

Cecil locked eyes with the woman. "I'll give you $300."

She gasped.

"I'll pay $400," Santa said.

"How about $500?" Cecil said.

"Okay, okay," Santa said. "I'll make it $600."

The woman burst into tears. She handed the microwave to Santa, took his money and rushed to the door. Santa and Cecil looked at each other for a second, grinning, before Cecil also headed for the door. The woman had climbed into a friend's car, and the friend was getting ready to back up. Cecil motioned for them to stop and roll down their windows. Santa, who followed a few steps behind Cecil, walked up to the car and addressed the seller of the battered microwave.

"Here," Santa said. "I've changed my mind. You can have the microwave back. Merry Christmas."

He didn't ask for his money. The woman quickly realized he didn't want it. New tears flowed. Her friend cried, too.

Cecil and Santa waved goodbye, got into their car and left.

Thirteen

Return to the Dixie Diner

Retired Mississippi diner owner Ted Horn baked several cakes in anticipation of receiving visitors from Kansas City.

A sweet aroma drifted through his kitchen as he pulled them from the oven in his modest ranch-style home. He lived on a well-manicured street in Tupelo, the birthplace of Elvis Presley.

It was a few days before Christmas 1999. A Missouri gentleman had called and said he was doing historical research on Chickasaw County, Mississippi. The gentlemen wanted to talk with Ted about the 27-seat diner he had operated for two decades in Houston, the Chickasaw County seat.

Though retired, the 81-year-old Ted still arose at 3:30 a.m., the time he used to wake so he could open the diner at 4:30 a.m., when a cadre of milk delivery drivers appeared for their morning coffee and grits. He'd close daily at 2 p.m. and head home to their farm to feed the cows and pigs and tend a large garden.

The tiny diner stood around the corner from the town square. Horn cooked, cleaned, served the food and rang up the tabs. A people person, he enjoyed meeting and talking with customers.

His wife, Ruby, had worked in the welfare department in Houston. Sometimes, she also baked pies for the diner. Now, having battled cancer and a broken hip and leg, she suffered from Alzheimer's at age 79. She sat in a chair as Ted frosted the cakes, put them on a table and sat down to wait for his guests. The couple's two children, David Horn and Sandra Cox, came by to listen.

Ted didn't know it, but the "researcher" actually was Santa, using the name Bill and disguising his voice. Santa wanted to learn if Ted Horn was the diner owner who helped Santa out of a jam in 1971. Santa longed to locate that diner owner, but he remembered only fuzzy details about what the man looked like. He never knew his name but had called him Cookie.

Once he gathered enough information about Ted Horn, Santa felt sure he'd found the person who changed his life.

He divulged his reunion plans to reporters from *The Kansas City Star* and KMBC Channel 9. They agreed to follow him to Mississippi.

When the doorbell first rang at the Horn household, his callers turned out to be Kansas City journalists. They asked if they could enter. Ted settled into a comfortable chair in the living room. The journalists shared the couch. One asked Ted about the diner days.

"We started in '61," Ted said. "It was in a different place then, the northeast corner of the square. In 1971, the man who owned the building sold it to the bank and we had to move to a little building behind Walgreens."

He featured home cooking: peas, potatoes, corn bread, salads, dessert. Regular grub, nothing fancy, Ted said.

For a while, Ted also ran a food truck and served sandwiches to factory workers. At one time, he posted a note: "If you are hungry and don't have money, if you will tell me, I'll give you something to eat. But please don't steal it."

Eventually, Ted leased out the diner and kept the food truck. Shortly after Ruby retired in 1985, Ted sold the truck and retired, too. They bought a little camper and started traveling.

"The old diner is a barber shop now," Ted said.

He held in his lap a national magazine with an article about Kansas City's Secret Santa. The article mentioned Santa receiving help in a Houston diner. Ted Horn pointed to the magazine. "That was my diner," he said.

The doorbell rang again. A rotund stranger entered.

"I'm looking for a fellow named Ted," the stranger said.

"That's me," Ted said from his chair.

"How ya doing?" the stranger asked, offering a handshake.

"For an old man," Ted answered, "I guess all right."

Santa took a deep breath and asked: Was Ted the man who had run that diner in Houston?

Ted nodded. "That's me."

"I'm that guy who was there 28 years ago," Santa said. "But I was a whole lot skinnier."

Horn, who had hoped to meet Secret Santa some day, smiled. He just had.

"I kinda figured you were," Ted said softly, "but I didn't know."

They talked about the diner, about Houston, about the food truck. Santa opened a large canvas bag and pulled out two books, a coffee cup, a Royals cap and Chiefs cap. He gave them to members of Ted's family.

"I wanted to come by and say, 'Thanks,' " Santa said.

"You're welcome," Ted answered. "I probably took your order, cooked it and brought it to you and took your money." He paused. "Well, I was going to take your money, but you didn't have any."

"I was going to take yours," Santa said.

Everyone laughed.

They talked about what the diner looked like, including its orange leather stools. They talked about the $20 Santa received, a large sum considering the times.

"What do you reckon that $20 is worth today?" Santa asked. "Do you know how to figure net present value? I had somebody figure that for me."

Before Santa could tell Horn the answer (roughly $120), Horn responded: "To me, that twenty-dollar bill then was probably like $10,000 to you today."

Santa hesitated. He hadn't expected Ted to say such a thing. He changed the topic briefly then returned to the money question and Ted's $10,000 answer.

"Funny you should say that number," Santa said as he pulled

out an envelope thick with hundred-dollar bills. "See what's in that envelope."

"I hope it's not *that* much money," Horn said. "You don't owe me nothing."

Ted examined the bills, which were wrapped in a paper band that said "$10,000."

"Good God," Ted said softly. "You didn't have to do this."

"But I wanted to," Santa said.

"I appreciate it," Ted said.

"You never know what one little act of kindness will do for somebody," Santa said. "It can change their whole life, and it changed mine. When I got out on the road after getting gas, I figured out what you did."

Santa's voice broke, and he stopped for a moment. The emotion he had tried to hide now bubbled to the surface. No one spoke.

"If it hadn't been for you," Santa continued, "I might have ended up in some jailhouse somewhere, because a hungry man sometimes will do desperate things."

As they watched, Ted's grown children grew teary eyed.

"I can't believe this," David said. "For this man to come down and do this for my father — it's almost more than we can bear. Right here at Christmas time — I think that's the spirit and meaning of Christmas."

His sister, Sandra, let it slip that her dad secretly had hoped for a visit from Secret Santa.

"When he first saw the (magazine) article, people started calling," she said. "When Bill started calling him about it, he was real excited. In the last week or so, he began to think the man might come. It means a whole lot. Not the money, just getting to meet the man."

Her dad, Sandra said, always tried to help people in need, such as hobos walking through the countryside. This was before he owned the diner, when Sandra was little.

"If they came to our house, Mommy and Daddy always fed them at a picnic table in the yard," she said.

Neither David nor Sandra was surprised to learn that their dad had helped Santa.

"My dad sensed that this man was in dire need and not faking it," David said. "My dad sensed that and didn't want to embarrass him."

It was just as Santa had thought in 1971 when he escaped Houston in his little stick-shift car.

Now that he'd met Ted again, Santa craved a sightseeing trip. He wanted to drive the 35 miles south to Houston to revisit the old town square. He had a "sleigh," better known as a red Ford Explorer, parked outside. Would Ted like to take a ride with him?

Ted grinned. "Sure."

As they pulled into the Houston square, memories flooded back. At the corner of Madison and North Jackson, Santa paused. That was where he had slept in his car, with the engine and heater running until the car drank its last swirl of gasoline.

Around the corner, the old Dixie Diner sign remained affixed atop what now was a barber shop. Inside, a barber offered cuts for $5 or shaves for $5.

They walked in and said hello.

"Right here," Ted said, pointing, "was the island. There were two booths here, a divider and two more booths there."

Ted reflected on the big breakfast Santa ordered in 1971. It probably would have cost about a buck-twenty-five.

"Back then, we sold a hamburger for a quarter and a cheeseburger for 30 cents."

Santa, Ted and the rest of the group drove across town and ate lunch at Moore's Restaurant. After finishing, Santa reached in his pocket for some cash and his usual tip money. The waitresses and cooks screamed in joy.

"Is it real?" Joyce Atkinson asked.

From there, Santa and Ted visited a laundry and a Sonic before returning to see the barber. Herbert Gregory, the owner, was cutting Malcolm Walters' hair. Santa handed out hundred-dollar bills. One recipient grinned and said, "Tell him he can come back any time."

On the return drive to Tupelo, Ted and Santa talked more. Watching Santa give out money had been a special treat for Ted.

"He was caught up in the excitement," Santa recalled later. "He didn't know how to react, or what he was supposed to do."

The adventure sapped Santa emotionally yet energized him physically.

"It was very difficult for me," he said. "I can't describe the feeling, but I suddenly started getting really peaceful while we were talking. I don't think it sunk in until about midnight, when I was by myself. I looked at those old pictures (of Houston) again and started to really feel good. I'm glad I did it.

"You never know. I just got an e-mail from a good friend. A close friend of his had died. He told me he really felt bad because he didn't have the opportunity to tell him how much he meant to him growing up."

Santa was glad he hadn't lost that opportunity with Ted Horn.

Back home after Santa left, Ted felt some of the same emotions. A child of the Depression, he stuck most of Santa's gift in a trust fund, after giving $500 to the Salvation Army. He felt that everyone should follow Santa's lead: get out and give.

Ten days after Christmas, he reached for a pad of writing paper. Addressing the letter to the newspaper reporter who had left her business card the day Santa visited, Ted began writing.

It has been so long since I have written a letter I don't know how this will turn out.... Words cannot express the way I feel. It is almost like a dream. Tell Santa I will forever be grateful for the gift. In my wildest dreams I never expected anything like that. In this age of angels, he is an angel in disguise. Thanks from the bottom of my heart...I can't put into words how it felt when he handed me the money. Thanks again to all of you and may God bless.

90

Fourteen

'I'll eat my hat'

Two days before Christmas in 1999, retired doughnut maker Jerry Brooks scoured the aisles of a Kansas City thrift store looking for bargains.

The lanky 69-year-old man in tattered clothes carried 75 cents in his pocket. If lucky, he could find something warm for less than that.

Eventually, Jerry settled on a winter scarf. The price: 45 cents.

As Jerry walked toward the checkout counter, a cheery stranger in a red flannel shirt brushed past. The stranger stopped briefly.

"Merry Christmas, sir," Santa said, thrusting a folded hundred-dollar bill into Jerry's hand.

"Merry Christmas," Jerry answered before looking at what he held. He gasped.

"He gave me $100. God! I can't believe that! Lor-r-r-d have mercy."

Jerry looked around the thrift store. In clothing aisles, shoe aisles and miscellaneous aisles, other people were examining crisp hundred-dollar bills.

"I don't know where he came from," Jerry said of Santa, "but if he doesn't live to be 500, I'll eat my hat!"

Fifteen

A fallen firefighter

A week before Christmas 1999, Kansas City lost a fire-fighter in a four-alarm warehouse blaze.

As the second battalion chief to arrive, John Tvedten drew the job of directing firefighting efforts inside the building. For 15 minutes or more, crews battled a fire that seemed to be coming under control. Suddenly, thick black smoke engulfed them, making it impossible to see.

Another chief suggested that the teams pull out. Answering into his radio, Chief Tvedten agreed. Dispatchers sounded emergency evacuation tones over the radios. Others sounded the air horns on the fire trucks.

Everyone withdrew safely except "Car 106," the radio call sign for John Tvedten.

Outside, six rescue teams formed. At one point, someone faintly heard the alarm bell ringing on John's air tank, signifying only five to seven minutes of air remained. Still, rescuers couldn't find the 47-year-old man.

Eventually, the ringing bell stopped. Everyone knew what that meant.

They finally found him sprawled on the floor 150 feet inside the building, where he had gotten lost in the heavy smoke. A 26-year department veteran, he was the first Kansas City firefighter to die fighting a blaze in 11 years.

Co-workers remembered that he remained calm and professional even as his air ran low. They remembered, too, how he had insisted that firefighters have the best equipment. He had criticized the city's underpowered emergency radio system, which threatened both police and firefighters when it failed to work, and he had fought for a better system. He drove all over the city, testing the radios. He cared about all aspects of a firefighter's life, from safety to pensions. He had recommended the department initiate "RIT" teams, or rapid intervention teams that would stand by during structure fires, immediately ready to enter the burning building to find a lost or trapped firefighter. Those teams didn't form in Kansas City, though, until after John Tvedten died.

An editorial in *The Kansas City Star* called him a hero.

John Tvedten spent a career thrilling to the excitement of attempting to suppress fires but knowing the deadliness the flames could bring, it said. *He died making the Fire Department safer for his colleagues and the city he served.*

John Tvedten's father, also a battalion chief, had died tragically, too — not fighting a fire, but as an off-duty husband enjoying a Friday night tea dance. He was inside the Hyatt Regency Hotel in Kansas City when two of its skywalks collapsed in July 1981, killing 114 people and sending the city into shock. It was the nation's worst structural failure disaster.

The younger Tvedten's service took place at Kemper Arena. Afterward, a procession of fire trucks drove past the city's Firefighters Memorial at 31st and Pennsylvania then past Station 32, where John had worked, and finally to the funeral home.

Firefighters set up a memorial fund at their credit union. It largely was intended as an educational fund for John's 11-year-old son, Tyler.

Christmas Eve morning, six days after John died and three days after the funeral, Santa and some elves headed to a fire station to donate to the memorial fund. But at the station, firefighters refused to take Santa's money. Instead, they asked that he give it directly to John's widow, Susan, who lived in a neighborhood not far away. One of the firefighters called the house. Susan was home. Yes, Secret Santa could come over with elves and firefighters, she said, but she asked that his group give her an hour first. Still in her night clothes, she wasn't ready for company.

When the group arrived, Susan's eyes locked on a face familiar to all of Kansas City: George Brett, the Hall of Fame third basemen and three-time batting champion who led the Kansas City Royals to a World Series championship in 1985. Santa and George had met at a charity golf tournament and become friends. This day, George was playing the role of Santa's elf.

Excitement over seeing George swirled through the adults in the house, including several of Susan's relatives. They shook George's hand. Too young to remember George's baseball feats, and not much of a baseball fan anyway, Tyler wasn't sure what to make of the fuss.

Santa cleared his throat.

"I'm so sorry to hear about your tragedy," he said. "We want to make things a little better this time of year."

George handed Tyler an autographed bat, other baseball memorabilia and a check toward the memorial fund. Santa gave $5,000, all in hundred-dollar bills. The firefighters agreed to take the money and the check and deposit them in the trust fund.

"Thank you," said Susan, who had heard of Secret Santa but knew little about him. To her, something special had just happened.

George Brett felt so, too. As he walked outside, an amazing feeling overcame him.

"I don't think I've ever felt so good about myself," he said later, "as I did that day."

SANTA'S SECRET: A STORY OF HOPE

Sixteen

Honoring a hero

Santa awoke and glanced at his clock. The digital numbers read 4:12 a.m., nearly two hours before his alarm was to sound.

Unable to sleep, he crawled from bed, scurried downstairs to his office and clicked on his computer.

For several years, Santa had attempted to find at least one special person to provide extra cash for the holidays. One year, it was the St. Joseph woman raising 12 children. Five years had passed since that day. Now, it was a December morning in 2000, and Santa had another special person in mind.

He had asked Kansas City firefighters for suggestions of whom to help. They had recommended Christina Thomas, whose husband had died in an October trench collapse as firefighters frantically fought to free him. A month later, a fire swept through her house, destroying her belongings. She and her son, Dakota, had resettled in an apartment in Liberty.

As Santa stared at his computer, an idea flashed through his head. He would craft a special certificate, named in honor of a fallen hero, and award it to Christina.

His hands moved swiftly over the keyboard. Words flowed. When everything looked just right, he turned on the printer, made color copies and studied his work. Yup, this would do just fine.

Hours later, on one of those bitterly cold Midwestern winter mornings, Santa pulled into a parking lot at the Liberty apartment complex. Three firefighters waited: Ray Wynn, Charlie Cashen and Carl Tripp. Santa had invited them to the presentation, which the young mother had been told would involve the fire department. The firefighters wore their uniforms and warm coats. They stomped their cold feet as Santa explained that he was going to give Christina money. He didn't mention the certificate, however.

Ray knocked on Christina's door and asked if the group could enter. She waved everyone inside timidly. Her mother already was there, visiting.

"I don't know if you all can fit in here," Christina said softly as person after person walked into the compact living room. Some rubbed their hands together, warming them from the outside chill.

After everyone squeezed in, Santa looked at the petite Christina and said: "We wanted to stop by. We have a certificate for you."

He opened a file folder, pulled out the certificate and began reading. Christina, he said, had been appointed a John Tvedten Angel, in honor of a Kansas City battalion chief who died inside a burning building the previous December.

The three firefighters gasped.

Carl couldn't swallow. Ray choked up. Charlie, who had been John Tvedten's driver, fought back tears.

Santa told Christina she had "the responsibility to pass on kindness to others in the same spirit it is given to you."

He opened a white envelope and handed her $5,000. Her chin quivered. A tear rolled down her left cheek. For a moment no one spoke. Then Santa asked the firefighters to sign the certificate before he gave it to Christina.

"God bless you," she said in a tiny voice that sounded as unsure as her wave had been when inviting the strangers inside. "Thank you."

Suddenly thrust into the role of single parent, she needed the money to pay bills first and take care of Christmas second. She hugged Santa. He and his "rookie" firefighter elves turned and headed back out into the frigid air. A reporter and photographer lingered.

"The fire department did so much when Michael was buried," Christina told them. "This is overwhelming. This is amazing. It will help me cope with everything that has happened."

Outside, the firefighters felt, just perhaps, even more overwhelmed.

Santa had never met John Tvedten. Having a complete stranger honor their fallen friend that way — well, they just couldn't believe it.

"That was one of the neatest things I've ever been included in," Carl said later.

"That is what Christmas is all about," Ray said.

Added Charlie: "I think (Santa) understood what John meant for us."

Perhaps, too, Santa felt drawn to John's son, Tyler, who became fatherless at age 11. Santa knew what it was like to grow up without a father.

Someone called Susan Tvedten.

"Guess what Santa just did," the caller said.

As she heard the story, Susan felt touched once again by Santa, this time for the special way he had honored her husband.

"It keeps John's name and memory alive," she said.

Seventeen

Avoiding eviction

Amanda Green reported to work at a Liberty gas and convenience store fretting about her landlord's plans to evict her and her two children, ages 8 and 6.

A customer approached to purchase a hot chocolate.

"That will be 52 cents," Amanda said.

The front door jingled. A man in a red flannel shirt entered.

"I had $15 in gas," said the man, who thrust a hundred-dollar bill toward Amanda. "Why don't you keep the change?"

She took the bill from his hand and opened the cash drawer.

"You're not serious," she said, looking down to pull smaller bills from the drawer. But Santa, who had just delivered his first Tvedten Angel award a few blocks away, turned and dashed for the door.

"Sir!" Amanda shouted after him, waving his change.

"Keep it," Santa said as he dashed into the frigid air.

"Sir!" Amanda yelled again, this time louder.

But Santa was gone.

Amanda looked at the $85 in her hand.

"Oh my gosh," she said. Her eyes moistened.

Some of Santa's elves remained in the store, watching Amanda. One stepped up to the counter.

"You ready for Christmas?" the elf asked before handing over another hundred-dollar bill. "Have a merry one."

"Oh my gosh," Amanda said. "What is going on?"

Tears spouted. "What's wrong?" a reporter standing nearby asked.

"They are supposed to file the eviction on me today," Amanda said. "I owe $400 and something. If I'm evicted, I don't know what I am going to do."

Though behind in her rent, she had used some of her income to buy Christmas gifts for her children, she explained. She didn't want them to miss out on the holiday.

The convenience store's front door jingled again. Sheriff Tom — out of his jurisdiction by one county, but nonetheless still providing security for Santa — stepped inside.

"Is it true you are in a little trouble?" Tom asked Amanda, who nodded, unable to speak.

He handed her four more rolled-up bills. "Merry Christmas," he said before darting back outside.

Amanda unrolled the money and burst into sobs. Her hands shook so severely that she was unable to ring up the next purchase. She backed away from the cash register and motioned a co-worker to take over.

"I don't know what to say," she said.

And she sobbed some more.

Eighteen

'It's Christmas at Ground Zero!'

The horrific video played over and over on televisions across America.

Terrorists flew passenger jets into both World Trade Center towers in New York and into the Pentagon outside Washington. The Trade Center towers collapsed separately into heaps of dust, debris, bodies and blood. Heroic passengers on a fourth jetliner perished in a Pennsylvania field after attempting to retake their cockpit from terrorists, who may have been aiming for the Capitol or the White House.

In the days following September 11, 2001, Santa walked around his Missouri home in a daze. Like the rest of America, he felt sick.

He mourned for the thousands of lives lost, for the families now suffering, for what other horrors future terrorists might attempt. He thought of the victims who might never be found and felt for their loved ones.

In the previous three years, he'd visited New York three times. He'd bought a baseball cap that read NYPD from a vendor near the Trade Center towers. He and his family had ridden one tower's elevator to the top and eaten at the Windows on the World restaurant.

After four days of moping, an idea struck: He should take Secret Santa money to Ground Zero in December. The Big Apple needed a big pick-me-up.

Sure, he'd taken Secret Santa on the road before, to his birth state of Mississippi. But he'd never carried that much cash in such a big city, where quick exits would be difficult in the crowds. Plus, he'd be on foreign turf. He wouldn't know his way around. He wouldn't know escape routes.

Still, he felt pulled to New York. He had to go.

A reporter from *USA Today* had asked months ago to accompany him for a story. He called her.

"How would you like to meet me in New York in December?" he asked.

"Sure," she said.

He also called a reporter at *The Kansas City Star.* Would *The Star* want to go along?

"Of course!" the reporter answered.

Santa deliberated over which elf to take. Watching the reaction of elves gave him an extra kick at Christmas, but it also helped him teach others about the joy of helping people. Who would enjoy this trip? Hmmm.

Eventually, Santa recruited Kansas City Fire Department Captain Ray Wynn, who had met Santa on earlier outings. Firefighters lost many of their own at Ground Zero. Though Ray served a community more than a thousand miles west of New York, he was a brother to the FDNY.

December came quickly.

As Santa packed, he felt uneasy — and not because he'd be flying so soon after September 11, with heightened security at airports and uncertainty among passengers buckled into their seats. Instead, he worried about how he would feel when he saw the lower Manhattan skyline without its majestic twin towers.

He and Ray walked into the Kansas City airport about an hour before their flight to Laguardia. Santa wore his NYPD cap. They checked some luggage at the Midwest Express counter and carried other pieces to the security checkpoint near the gate.

Santa had stowed tens of thousands of dollars, all in hundred-dollar bills, inside zippered pockets of his photography vest, a light-tan piece of clothing fashioned with multiple places to put film, lenses and other gear. His carry-on bag bulged with goodies, including a red Santa hat.

He placed the bag on a conveyer belt and watched it disappear through the X-ray machine. He emptied his pockets of change and keys and walked through the metal detector to await his bag, but it didn't come out right away. The security screener studied the bag's image on his X-ray video screen and whispered something to a co-worker.

Santa had neglected to completely empty the bag before packing it. He'd accidentally left inside a metal golf pick used to fix dented greens.

The second security agent asked Santa to find and discard the pick.

Santa pulled out a few items, including the Santa hat, and piled them on a table. He reached inside and felt for the pick among the remaining items but couldn't find it. His fingers traced along the seams and into the bag's corners. Where was that darn pick? Seconds grew into minutes.

Santa glanced over his shoulder. The line of passengers had lengthened. They waited for him to clear the screening area.

A nervous flutter rolled through Santa's stomach. What if the security officers asked to search everything? What about his vest with all the money? What would they think about all of those hundred-dollar bills?

Santa laughed nervously and pulled more items from his carry-on bag. Finally, he saw the pick.

"There," he said, grabbing it and handing it to the security agent.

His muscles relaxed. He repacked quickly and headed to rows of seats near the gate, where a reporter and photographer from *The Star* read the newspaper as they waited. They had watched him unpack and repack, and they teased him about holding up the line. Santa shook his head.

"For a minute there," he said, "I thought I might have to call a friend at the FBI to get through."

On board, Santa slid into a seat next to Ray. He ordered cranberry juice and struck up conversations with the flight attendants.

"You from Kansas City?" he asked one.

"Overland Park," she said.

Santa turned to Ray and, talking loud enough for the flight attendant to hear, asked: "Have you heard about that man who goes around giving away money?"

"Yeah," Ray said, playing along. "I have."

"I've always wanted to do that, to give away money like that," Santa said, smiling.

"Do it," Ray said. "Just do it. You only live once."

Later, as the plane drew closer to New York, Santa motioned to the attendant.

"I've been watching how hard you all work," he told her, "so for Christmas, I'm going to buy you all dinner."

He handed over three hundred-dollar bills, one for each attendant. She scurried up the aisle to her co-workers and distributed their gifts. They whispered. She pointed to Santa.

The giddy attendants wrote a thank-you note and brought Santa a bottle of champagne.

"That was very sweet of you, sir," one told him.

After arriving at the airport, Santa, Ray and the journalists met Victor, a Ukrainian native who would be Santa's driver the next two days — and get a nice tip, too. Victor escorted them to a gray van and loaded luggage in the back.

Later that afternoon, near their mid-Manhattan hotel, Santa and Ray met up with *USA Today's* crew and two New York police officers. Shadows from towering skyscrapers dappled the sidewalks. Pedestrians, taxi-cabs and buses competed for space on bustling avenues. Horns honked, brakes squealed and exhaust fumes muddied the air.

Santa explained his game plan to uniformed officers Bruce Arch and Robert Amrhein.

"We want to go where there are people really hurting, people on the street, people out of work," he said. "I walk up to people, say 'Merry Christmas,' give them a hundred-dollar bill and I'm gone."

The officers nodded.

The group headed to an area where people applied for Medicaid cards and other assistance. Santa watched for people entering and leaving the assistance centers, but there was little traffic.

He spotted and walked toward a 51-year-old homeless man, who saw Santa's NYPD hat and thought he'd been busted for something. Santa gave him $200.

Not far away, a Federal Express delivery man unloaded boxes. Santa handed him $100.

"Is this a prank?" the delivery man asked. "This has never happened to me."

A young woman with children bundled in strollers walked past. Santa gave her money, too. Then he handed cash to a legless man in a wheelchair, another homeless man and a father walking with his son.

Their reactions were more subdued than Santa normally saw back in Kansas City. In that first hour, no recipient shouted. None cried. None jumped for joy. Instead, several looked at Santa as if he were crazy. Sometimes, when Santa stuck out his hand with a crumpled, almost hidden bill inside, people shook their heads and tried to turn it down.

One recipient looked at the cameras pointed at him and asked, "Is this a David Letterman joke?"

A woman wearing red studied the bill Santa had handed her, saw a police officer standing on a street corner and walked briskly toward him.

"Here," she told the officer as she held the bill near his face. "Some guy gave me this. It must be fake."

The officer examined the hundred.

"No," he said. "It's okay."

A 32-year-old mother clutched a Santa bill and smiled. She said she was going to buy her nine-month-old son "a big old toy."

"I think he's very generous," she said of Santa, adding that his gift was "so unlike New York."

Then she paused.

"Ever since 9/11, a lot of people have changed," she said.

Darkness arrived by 5 p.m., but activity still swirled on the streets and sidewalks. Santa headed for the heart of a ritzy shopping district along Seventh Avenue. Shoppers scurried past, lugging packages in one hand and cradling cell phones in the other. They didn't need his money, Santa knew. Yet, inspired by a classic movie, Santa wanted to create his own miracle near the Macy's department store at the corner of 34th Street and Seventh Avenue.

A Salvation Army bell-ringer stood on the sidewalk, pumping his hand. A familiar ding-ding, ding-ding, ding-ding resonated from his bell. Santa dropped a Ben Franklin into his kettle.

Santa paused and glanced to his right. A young man stood at one of Macy's doors wearing a jacket that said "Security." James Fraizer, a 19-year-old from Harlem, had started the job three weeks earlier.

Santa walked up to him and asked, "Do you work at Macy's?"

James nodded.

Santa asked a couple more questions and learned that James had a young child. Santa reached into a pocket.

"I was told to come by and see you," Santa said. "Merry Christmas."

He slipped James a folded bill.

"Why are you giving me this?" James asked as he studied the bill. But when he looked up, the stranger already had dashed into the Manhattan night. Two reporters stared at him.

"I'm shocked," James said. "I'm just shocked. He just gave me $100. I am completely shocked. Is he Santa Claus? He looks like Santa Claus. I guess he might be. I believe in Christmas now."

James explained that he'd stopped believing in Santa Claus after he turned 10. Now he felt that maybe, just maybe, he had been wrong to quit believing. Now, he could buy his month-old son more things for Christmas.

"Tell Secret Santa thank you," James said. "Have a happy New Year."

At the next corner, Santa already had locked onto his next target: two men in white uniforms pulling a tall blue plastic trash can. The maintenance workers had paused for traffic to clear before crossing a street. Santa walked up, looked into the trash can and exclaimed: "How in the world did you possibly miss that! You guys better be more careful!"

He pulled two hundred-dollar bills from the trash and handed one to each surprised man. Adrian Camacho, a 62-year-old from the Bronx, said it took him 11 years on the job to reach $11.48 in hourly wages.

"This is a shock, to see this amount of money," he said.

As the reporters talked to Camacho, Santa retreated the way he came, to a safe spot in front of Macy's where he could watch the reaction of people around the trash can.

Word spread quickly that two men had found money in the trash. One man walked past Santa wearing a stunned expression and said, "Someone just left $5 million in the trash."

Santa laughed. Rumors sure grow quickly in New York.

The reporters rejoined him. Soon, the teenaged security guard from Macy's walked toward Santa holding cookies he had gotten from the Salvation Army bell-ringer. He stretched his hand toward Santa.

"These are for you," he said.

Santa smiled and accepted the treats.

"You're supposed to give Santa milk and cookies," James said as he walked away, "but I ain't got no milk."

Later, outside a Port Authority transit terminal, Santa spotted 34-year-old Tony Franks-el from the Bronx walking with two bags in his hands.

"You dropped this," Santa said, sliding him a folded bill.

Tony's mouth fell open. It had to be a joke, he figured. But he could use the money.

"This is just a shock. I'm walking along, minding my own business…. Now I know what they mean when they say pennies from heaven. He's just a stranger passing out money?"

That's right, the two reporters assured him.

"No strings attached?"

No.

"This is no hoax?"

No. This was real.

Inside the Port Authority, Santa handed $300 to a man recently released from a New Jersey hospital. The man wanted to get home to Alabama for Christmas but lacked cash for the bus fare.

The two officers escorted Santa behind the terminal, to a dingy alley where homeless people gathered. Some stood, some sat in doorways and others stretched out on the pavement. One man smoking a cigar said he was from Florida. Santa gave him three bills. The man promised that he would go to "an agency," get a job and look for a place to live.

Others said they'd use Santa's money for food. One woman said she was from Kansas City. "No pictures, no pictures," she said as she gave Santa a big hug.

Suddenly, other homeless persons began to stir from dark corners and stoops. Words spread. Fearing a mob, the officers whispered to Santa and nodded to the terminal doors. The group raced back inside and almost trotted through the concourse toward the front doors. Two or three homeless men gave chase.

"Sir!" one shouted. "I heard you was giving Christmas gifts."

"I was," Santa said, feeling uneasy and unsafe. "Sorry."

Flanked by the officers, Santa hustled out front to the waiting van. The homeless men watched him go.

By now, the two officers had caught the Christmas spirit.

"I think it's great he is doing this for New York," said Bruce, who worked 12-hour shifts for nearly six weeks after the terrorist attacks. "We could really use it. I'll never forget this."

§ § §

The next morning, Santa's New York adventure turned south — toward lower Manhattan. Victor drove.

As they drew close to Ground Zero, Ray and Santa noticed an unobstructed expanse of blue sky overhead. Normally in this financial and shipping district, the massive twin towers cast long shadows on pedestrians and automobiles while limiting the view of the sky. Not anymore.

Escorted by representatives from the New York Senate, Santa's driver guided the van past the Chelsea Piers and parked near a sign that said, "Emergency vehicles only." Van doors popped open. Santa and Ray slipped out, crossed the street and rounded a corner. They spotted a makeshift memorial and walked over to investigate. Teddy bears and flower bouquets flanked hand-written messages left by mourners.

Firefighters in Japan are with you in spirit, one read.

Another began, *Dear Uncle Kenny. I miss you so much that I prayed for you at church.*

They stared silently for several minutes then walked around the block toward another memorial. Here, pictures of deceased firefighters lined a low wall.

"So many," Santa said softly, "and so many families."

The group walked around a corner and up a ramp onto a wooden platform overlooking Ground Zero. Visitors had scribbled or carved thousands of messages on the hand-rails.

Dear Billy. Thank you for 25 years of love, patience and humor, one said.

Workers erected the platform over what had been a large mud pile, the place from where Mayor Rudolph Giuliani delivered speeches after the towers collapsed. The platform allowed an impressive view of the gaping hole, still packed with melted metal, crumbled concrete and broken boards. The debris field once towered four stories high. Much of it had been cleared above street level, but a pit below held more. The day before, while Santa spread money in mid-Manhattan, workers at Ground Zero had uncovered a crumpled Ladder 4 fire truck four levels below the street.

Santa removed his ball cap. He and Ray leaned against the platform's waist-high railing and stared silently at the work scene below.

Large cranes and other machinery grunted while lifting chunks of mangled debris. Heavy dump trucks rumbled away, taking debris toward the piers. Dust drifted in the air.

Nearby, part of Building No. 6 still stood, its ugly frame twisted and discolored like something from a war movie. A dog trained to sniff out human bodies trotted past with its handler. Booties protected its paws.

A stale odor permeated the air.

"That's what death smells like," Santa said.

He had wondered how he would feel when he reached this site. Now he knew. He was angry — very angry at those terrorists.

Sad, too.

"It makes me want to go home and hug my family," he said.

Ray pulled a camera from a pocket and snapped a picture.

After a few somber minutes, the group sauntered back down the platform and walked to the van. Victor circled the debris field, weaving through streets cluttered with big trucks, to reach the opposite side. He parked. Santa's escorts took him down a block and around the corner, where workers swarmed in and out of a historic Episcopal chapel. Open around the clock, St. Paul's provided free meals for the workers, many of whom also napped there. More than 200 years earlier, George Washington had worshipped at St. Paul's.

Security remained tight; privacy for the workers remained a priority. "Wait here," one of the escorts told the news photographers with Santa. "Photographs aren't allowed."

Inside, letters, banners and schoolchildren's notes from across the country plastered every wall and pew. Workers had stored boxes and boxes of more notes and letters in the balcony.

In September, Giuliani had called the chapel a miracle because it didn't lose as much as a window when the World Trade Center complex collapsed across the street.

Santa asked to speak to the priest.

"Where does one make a donation?" he inquired.

They walked into the sacristy. Santa reached into his vest pocket and pulled out a large wad of hundred-dollar bills.

"Oh my gosh!" the Rev. Lyndon Harris exclaimed as he clutched his hand over his chest. "It's Christmas at Ground Zero!"

The two reporters mentioned that their photographers were outside. Couldn't they come in for this? Please?

Finally, someone said yes. An escort fetched the photographers.

When Santa finished counting, $5,000 lay on the sacristy counter, enough for volunteers to feed workers for about two days.

"Who is Secret Santa?" Father Lyndon asked.

"Nobody," someone said.

"Obviously, we are elated and very grateful," Father Lyndon said. "Oh my gosh. I'm blown away."

Outside afterward, Santa asked his escorts what had happened to the people who ran small businesses in the area. Many shops had closed for weeks or months, they said. Owners were struggling to pay rent.

Santa walked down one block and ducked into stores that had reopened. He gave money to the owner of a shoe repair shop, bought six hats from a street vendor and handed out Ben Franklins to workers in a clothing store, where a front display window, untouched since September 11, showed how deep ashen dust had settled after the towers collapsed.

Santa chatted with missionary volunteers at a prayer station then trotted into a small drug store.

"I'm so thirsty I'd give $100 for a bottle of water," he told the clerk.

"It's 89 cents," the clerk answered.

"No," Santa said, "It's $100. Merry Christmas."

Outside, Santa picked up a $4 pair of earmuffs from a street vendor then handed him $100.

"What!" the vendor exclaimed. "We have no change."

"Keep it," Santa said.

After a long walk, Santa's crew approached a fire station, home to Engine 5 and Ladder 15. Flowers, notes and pictures filled a memorial outside that honored 14 fallen firefighters. Black and blue bunting draped the top of it. Santa read the names and the banners and studied the wreaths and flowers. *God bless the bravest FDNY,* one sign said.

He went inside and asked to speak to the captain. After a brief conversation, Santa left $1,000 for the New York Police and Fire Widows and Children's fund. The captain put the money in an envelope.

"Thank you for coming," he said.

"You're welcome," Santa answered.

After a meal break, Santa spotted a dry-cleaners. He ducked inside.

"Merry Christmas," he announced and held out a Ben Franklin.

"No, no, no," the owner said, waving off the money. Santa pushed it closer. "It's okay," he said.

"I cannot," the man answered.

"Do you believe in Santa Claus?" Ray asked.

"I believe, but I cannot take the money," the man said.

"You can give it to someone who needs it," Santa suggested.

The man refused to budge. "No, no," he said again.

Santa looked at Ray and shrugged. He tucked the money back in his pocket, wished the man a "Merry Christmas," turned and walked out. Ray followed.

"That's okay," Santa said. "We can find someone else."

Sure enough. Around the corner, a 51-year-old man stood talking on a pay phone. Santa stooped down as if to pick up something.

"This must be yours," he told the man, who was named David. "It was laying right here."

"You've got to be kidding me," David said, hanging up the phone. He studied Santa's face. Santa grinned.

"I'll take it," David said. "Thank you, but I've got no idea what's going on."

Santa started to walk away. A reporter asked the man, "What do you think about that?"

"He made me happy," David answered. "Christmas is coming and I'm between jobs."

Santa suddenly stopped. His ears had caught a phrase that struck a chord. *Christmas is coming, and I'm between jobs.* Santa turned back and handed the man a second hundred-dollar bill.

"Well, God bless us all," David said. "I had $6.25 in my pocket to buy a combo platter. Words fail me. As a New Yorker, I'm so prepared to be put on or jinxed or joked. That's the most unabashed thing I've ever seen. My friends and relatives aren't going to believe it."

Santa chuckled. He'd heard that before.

Nineteen

A close call in Manhattan

After two days of spreading money through Manhattan, Santa awoke the final morning of his trip with only a few plans before heading to the airport.

He wanted to buy souvenirs for family at a Fire Department gift shop. He also planned to donate to a mid-Manhattan social services agency that helped people who lost their jobs following the terrorist attacks.

That morning, the story of his New York visit played on the front covers of both *USA Today* and *The Kansas City Star*. One paper's picture showed him from behind, walking down a New York sidewalk. The other showed his backside as he stared at a memorial display for fallen firefighters.

USA Today's crew had gone home, but a reporter and photographer from *The Star* remained. They also planned to fly back to Kansas City that afternoon and decided to accompany Santa to the airport.

Shortly after the group finished browsing at an FDNY gift shop, the *Star* photographer's cell phone rang. Bill Dalton, an editor back in Kansas City, reported that the newsroom switchboard had been lit up all morning with calls from national media and others who had heard about Santa's New York adventure. *The New York Post,* CNN, the BBC and others wanted to interview Santa.

The photographer lowered the phone and reported the developments.

"What do you want to do?" the reporter asked.

Color drained from Santa's face. In Kansas City, he gave interviews only to journalists he trusted. If a television station didn't abide by his rules — such as how much of him they could show on the air — he didn't let them follow him again. Now, national media wanted to interview him. He didn't know them, and he feared any situation that could expose his identity.

"Maybe I'll do a radio interview later," he said.

The photographer scribbled contact information for the BBC and handed it to Santa.

Victor dropped the group about a block from The Lambs, the social service agency Santa planned to help. He'd saved $5,000 for the organization, which already had received shipments of toys from Heart-to-Heart International, a charity based in the Kansas City suburb of Olathe, Kansas.

Parked just outside The Lambs, a television cameraman and reporter from a New York NBC affiliate waited in an NBC van. From clues gleaned in *The Kansas City Star* and *USA Today*, they had deduced which agency Santa planned to visit. When they saw a group of four persons, including one carrying large cameras, walking their way, they figured they had found him. The reporter jumped from the van and approached Santa.

"Are you Secret Santa?" he asked.

Santa stopped, studied the man's face and glanced at the news van on the curb. Rats. He hadn't expected this. He didn't know what to say, so he didn't say anything.

"Are you Secret Santa?" the reporter asked again. "Are you from Kansas?"

Santa didn't live in Kansas. He lived in Missouri.

"No," Santa said in answer to the Kansas question. "Uh, we're, uh, looking for some barbeque."

The television reporter pointed to a restaurant the foursome had passed a few doors back. Santa thanked him, spun faster than a Midwestern tornado and trotted back to the restaurant. It hadn't opened yet for lunch, so the group ducked inside a restaurant next door instead. Santa let out a deep breath.

"Whew!" he said. "That was close."

They sat at a table and ordered soft drinks while Santa pondered what to do. After a few minutes, Santa conjured a plan. He'd send Ray back up the street with the money. He came up with the idea while Ray was gone to the restroom and unavailable to protest. Santa laughed. That's what Ray got for leaving.

When Ray returned, Santa explained his plan then called Victor to pick him up in the van. He would meet the rest of the group around the block, after Ray delivered the gift. Ray nervously took an envelope from Santa. He'd never carried that much cash.

"You give the lady the money," Santa said. "All you've got to say is, 'I'm a Kansas City firefighter. I'm Santa's elf.'"

Ray nodded, though he looked like he wanted to hide. He tucked the envelope inside his jacket.

Santa handed Ray a red Santa hat and asked him to wait a few minutes. The reporter and photographer headed up the street to get in position for pictures and interviews.

The Lambs handed out 5,000 toys a day to needy families, an administrator told the reporter. "We've got huge lines," she said. "We definitely need everything we have. Already, there are 80,000 people without work and there probably will be another 30,000 by the end of this month."

On the curb, workers unloaded a delivery truck. The boxes were stamped, "Heart to Heart International." The agency's donations filled an entire section inside the store.

Ray walked up the sidewalk, up The Lambs' stairs and into the building. The Kansas City reporter and photographer followed. The NBC crew, still inside the station's van, somehow missed his arrival. Ray spoke briefly with an administrator. Though Ray said he was an elf, the administrator misunderstood and thought he was Secret Santa. The group stepped outside with the $5,000.

"Bless you," the administrator said, hugging Ray. "Thank you so much."

The NBC crew bolted from the van toward Ray and his red Santa hat. Questions flew.

"Can I see?" the cameraman asked, pointing his lens at the cash for a close-up.

With the cameraman briefly distracted, Ray took off down the street, his red hat bobbing among coat-clad people jostling on the crowded sidewalk. Seconds later, the NBC crew followed. Ray rounded a busy corner, stepped into a doorway and pulled off the red hat. Tucking it inside his jacket, he leaned forward and peered around the door frame to scour the street for the van. Inside the van, Santa watched as the NBC crew looked up and down the sidewalk, but they had lost Ray. Looking dejected, the NBC crew turned back toward The Lambs.

In the van, Santa opened a door for Ray, who climbed inside.

"What a rush!" Ray said.

The Kansas City photographer and reporter rejoined them. The photographer's phone rang again.

This time, Mayor Rudolph Giuliani wanted to meet Secret Santa, an editor back in Kansas City said.

A stunned Santa looked at his watch. He had to get to the airport. There simply wasn't time.

He had expected New York to be different. He was right.

Twenty

'See what you have done!'

After returning home from New York, Santa clicked on his computer to check e-mail arriving at his new e-mail address, which *USA Today* and *The Star* had published.

In previous years, many newspaper readers and television viewers had wanted to contact Santa but didn't know how, so they wrote or called the journalists who covered him. Some sent letters explaining a friend's dire situation and pleading for help. Others simply thanked Santa for inspiring them.

Today would be different. For the first time, people could contact him directly. Santa typed his password, opened his e-mail and looked at the spot where the tally of new messages appeared. It read: 579.

"Wow," Santa whispered.

He scanned the message lines. "You're an angel." "Reason to continue believing." "Thank you."

Santa opened one.

You have brought the spirit of Christmas to our city that is still reeling from 9/11. I am a Catholic priest in a midtown parish and you have renewed in me a faith in our humanity and in its Creator. I bless your kindness and promise to remember you in my prayers...

It was signed, "Father Kevin."

Santa opened another e-mail. A woman told how she was reading a news article about him and bawling her eyes out. She admired his willingness to help and hoped to be successful enough someday to share her money with the world.

Someone named George from Idaho wrote that Santa's story hit home, not just because of the giving, but because of how Santa did it, without making people feel as if they were a charity case. George promised to do his part to help others.

A resident of Lyndonville, New York, told how three co-workers saved $2 apiece each month to buy gifts for needy families at Christmas. Because of Santa, they had decided to increase that amount to $5 a month.

A flight attendant from London called his story one of the most uplifting she'd ever read. Anna in Maryland said his story reminded her of the true meaning of Christmas. A 17-year-old high school student in Allentown, Pennsylvania, explained that his economics teacher had asked his students to read the article, and the whole class was shocked by Santa's kindness, especially because so many people in the world who are blessed with money never think of sharing it with people less fortunate. *So, on behalf of my class and myself, thank you for being so sweet and kind-hearted.*

Many of the e-mails didn't contain home addresses, so Santa couldn't tell where they originated. Others said they were from West Virginia, Maryland or Michigan. One person sent an e-mail from Turkey. Santa looked at the Turkish words and shook his head. He would need help reading that one.

Nearly all of the e-mails mentioned emotions that his actions had stirred.

Brad reported that he had tears streaming down his face. Walter said he cried, even though, as a macho man, he wasn't supposed to admit that. Kent said he read the article to his wife and three sons in tears.

The year had been difficult for them, Kent said. Though they had a tree, no presents sat beneath it. Yet the article showed them that giving, rather than receiving, was the answer. Kent blessed Santa.

A Tennessee man said that Santa's story would change his life. He said he was headed to New York to visit his brother and sister-in-law in Queens. After he returned home, he promised to become more involved in Chattanooga and start attending church again. *I have never heard of anything like you are doing and I think it is the most beautiful thing ever done in this crazy world. You have completely inspired me and restored my faith in humanity and GOD.*

Someone named Barb typed just a short note: *All it takes is one special person to remind us no matter how terrible we think things are, there is always someone who is more in need. Thanks for the adjustment. Keep doing great things.*

And from somewhere in cyberspace, Rachel gigged Santa for his modesty. *I understand from the story that you are embarrassed by accolades. Well, too bad! You deserve a HUGE thank you for what you have done and continue to do. You are an inspiration for the rest of us to stop complaining that we are "poor" and "unfortunate" when we are truly overwhelmed by God's blessings. May God bless you, and happy holidays to you and your family.*

Santa needed a break. He backed away from the computer and gazed out his front window, at the dormant brown grass and naked trees. Winter had transformed his front yard's park-like landscape into a dreary dullness. Yet, this late-December day didn't feel at all dreary.

He had hoped that his giving would inspire others to do the same. This response overwhelmed him.

Day after day, e-mails arrived by the dozens. Many senders professed to be longtime followers of his Kansas City escapades and looked forward to reading his story every year. Some said they often handed out $5 or $10 to the needy. Many wished they could do more.

Over and over, they thanked him and called him an inspiration.

Santa wrote replies to as many people as he could. He thanked them for being kind and generous, too.

He forwarded some of their messages to the reporters who wrote about him with a note: *See what you've done!*

One wrote back: *No, Santa. See what **you** have done!*

The day after Christmas, Santa opened another e-mail and smiled. It came from David Horn, the son of retired Dixie Diner owner Ted Horn.

We have all seen the news reports by national media including CNN, USA Today and even heard same on CNN Radio. Your generosity in New York was, I am sure, most appreciated. All of these news items quote you as giving the credit to the owner of a small diner in Mississippi who helped you in 1971. It is utterly amazing that one small act of kindness valued at $20.00 would result in your benevolence of thousands and thousands of dollars to needy individuals. On behalf of my father, a good and generous man if there ever was one, and his family, allow me to offer a heartfelt THANK YOU!!!!!!! I pray God's blessing on you and yours. Happy 2002! Sincerely, David C. Horn.

Twenty-one
'You made Santa cry'

Two years after Santa surprised three Kansas City firefighters by naming an award after their fallen battalion chief, the firefighters concocted a way to thank him. They chose a unique gift, one no one could buy at a store.

As the day for presenting the surprise neared, one of the firefighters tipped off the Kansas City reporters who followed Santa each year. "Be sure to come to the fire station Friday," he told them by phone. "You won't want to miss this."

As usual, Santa had sought suggestions for families to help at Christmas. The firefighters selected a mother who had lost two young sons in a house fire six months earlier. They asked her to bring along family members and come to the fire station at 49th and Main on Friday morning.

That morning, Santa met up with one of his special elves: Buck O'Neil, a former Negro Leagues baseball star beloved by Kansas Citians. A tall twig of a fellow who flashed giant smiles as often as most people blinked, Buck had reached 90 but looked younger. His wit and storytelling skills still entertained many. Santa loved handing Buck a few bills and watching people flock to him as he dispensed the cash along with hugs and smiles, which people seemed to enjoy even more than the money.

As Buck and Santa joined up, Ray and Charlie and the other firefighters met at the station. Susan and Tyler Tvedten arrived early, as did some of the firefighters' spouses. They squeezed into a small office and took turns examining Santa's gift, which sat on a desk.

"Wow, that's beautiful," one said.

When the family to be honored arrived, the firefighters walked into the station's spacious truck bay, with its high ceilings and concrete floor. They chatted with the family next to a pumper truck until Santa arrived wearing a fake beard and Santa hat. Buck strolled behind him.

"Hello everyone," Santa said in a robust voice.

"Hi there, Santa," Ray and others answered.

Santa approached the guest family.

"You're probably wondering why the fire department got you out here," he said. "Each year, we choose somebody special to honor on behalf of a battalion chief who gave his life helping others. We call it the John Tvedten Angel award."

He held up a certificate printed on glossy paper.

"You are hereby appointed as one of John's angels, and with that comes an honorarium," he said.

He pointed to an envelope. "In here," he said, "is $2,500." He handed it to Shannon DeLapp, the woman whose sons had died. Family members gasped. Firefighters applauded.

"Oh, Lord," Shannon said. "God bless you."

Paula Russell watched from a few feet away. She had been baby-sitting Shannon's two sons, ages 5 and 3, the day they died. Shannon really needed the money, Paula said.

"Now maybe she can buy a headstone," Paula said softly.

Buck gave Shannon a warm hug and then Buck and Santa stepped back and let the journalists interview her.

"It's going to help a lot," Shannon said. "It will help pay bills."

The firefighters and Susan moved about 20 paces away. Now it was their turn. They motioned for Santa and Buck to join them.

Santa walked over. Thirteen-year-old Tyler held up the firefighters' gift: a leather firefighter's helmet adorned with a hand-painted helmet shield. Set on a white background, the shield featured a graceful white angel with white wings. A small fire hydrant, ladder and axe filled spaces beside and above the angel. Bold letters across the top of the shield said "Tvedten." More letters across the bottom said,

"Angel."

"This is from Susan, Tyler and the fire department," Ray explained.

Santa traced his hand over the fine leather brim and studied the artful shield. No one had ever done anything like this for him.

He melted.

"Awww," Buck said. "You made Santa cry."

For once, it was Santa's turn.

Twenty-two

Bonnie's Boots

Every minute, the lunch crowd in the tiny Town Topic eatery grew until customers claimed every stool along a counter running the length of the box-like diner at 20th and Broadway in Kansas City.

Arriving customers stood as they waited for stools to empty.

Town Topic packs a grill, office, supply room, counters and stools into a space smaller than many trailer homes. It serves true "fast food," meaning the workers cook it fast while the customers watch. There's no drive-through window. Finding a place to park outside can be as difficult as finding an open stool inside.

This December 2001 day, the entry door jingled often. One man whose truck had stalled just outside Town Topic's door asked if anyone could loan him a pair of jumper cables. The restaurant manager offered his.

Employees scurried about, taking orders on small pads, wiping counters, refilling coffee. Plates and serving ware clinked. The aroma of grilled hamburgers and fried onions wafted through the air as food sizzled on the grill.

When one plump customer with a short grayish-white beard stood to pay, he motioned to get the manager's attention.

"How many people do you have working today?" the plump customer asked.

"Five."

Santa reached into his pocket and counted five bills.

"Will you give each one of your employees one of these?" he asked, handing over $100 for each worker.

"My goodness!" the manager exclaimed.

Santa smiled and turned for the door.

A murmur rippled through the crowd.

"Where did this guy come from?" someone asked.

As the manager distributed the cash, tears welled up in waitress Theresa Lucas' eyes. "It's wonderful," she said. "Right now, I'm speechless."

Waitress Bonnie Gooch sobbed. Unable to compose herself, she ducked into a back room, where tears cascaded down her cheeks and her body shook. When she returned minutes later, she could barely speak. Her cheeks still glistened.

"My husband's got cancer," Bonnie whispered as more tears bubbled. "I need it real bad. He (Santa) sure was my angel."

Her husband, Tom, liked cowboy boots. The black pair he donned every day had holes growing in the soles. Bonnie wanted to buy him a new pair for Christmas, but she hadn't been able to afford it. Their finances had grown tight in the two months Tom had been battling a quick-growing cancer. Instead of driving big rigs, as the trucker had done for years, he now endured radiation treatments and heavy worries about the future.

She and Tom had been married less than a year when doctors diagnosed the cancer. Now Bonnie could give him the Christmas he wanted.

The next day, she shopped until she found the perfect pair: black boots with silver toes and silver on the heels.

Christmas morning, she waited until Tom had opened his other presents then handed him the surprise.

Weak from his treatments, Tom opened the box slowly. Tears welled in his eyes when he saw what was inside. They welled in Bonnie's eyes, too.

"It really meant a lot to me," she said later.

Twenty-three

After the snipers

An acquaintance called Mike Ross at his Baltimore office and asked if he could help arrange security for Secret Santa's visit to suburban Washington, D.C.

Secret Santa?

"Who's that?" asked Mike, supervisor of the FBI's violent crime squad in Baltimore.

The caller, retired FBI agent Larry McCormick, explained that Santa gave away tens of thousands of dollars each December, usually in the Kansas City area. Larry had met Santa years earlier, while Larry was assigned to the FBI's Kansas City office.

"Santa went to New York last year," Larry explained, summarizing Santa's trip to Ground Zero after the terrorist attacks.

This year, while watching news coverage of the October sniper attacks, Santa felt called to help people in and around Washington. The snipers had stalked the nation's capital and its suburbs for more than three weeks. They killed 10 persons, wounded three others and terrified thousands before authorities closed in, issued a description of their car and received a tip from an alert trucker who spotted the car at a rest stop.

Mike, who helped direct the sniper investigation, usually dealt with the seedier side of people. Helping Santa would be just the opposite — and it sounded like fun.

"Sure," Mike told Larry. "I can do that."

Mike called law enforcement officials in Prince George and Montgomery counties in Maryland and explained the request.

"What a great idea," one said.

131

Larry, meanwhile, called other FBI friends in the District of Columbia to set up security there.

A week before Christmas, Santa flew into the nation's capital carrying $25,000 and accompanied by a Kansas City television crew. Larry flew in from Arizona to serve as Santa's driver. Their schedule was packed. Santa would spend the first afternoon and evening in the capital before heading to Maryland the next morning to meet with Mike Ross and others. After handing out money there, the group would go to Virginia. Along the way, journalists from *USA Today* and *The Kansas City Star* would meet them.

After checking in at his D.C. hotel, Santa walked outside to start work. Several police cars and five or six officers waited, along with an assistant director from the FBI. They had taken up all the parking spaces out front.

"Oh, my goodness," Santa said.

As Larry introduced Santa to his security detail, passers-by stopped and stared. Santa had a feeling he'd have to change hotels. He was drawing too much attention. He leaned close to his buddy.

"Hey, Larry," he said. "You think you got enough officers here?"

Larry looked around.

"I think I overdid it," he admitted.

After finishing introductions, they loaded up and headed out. The patrol cars followed Larry and Santa in the van. Like a scout tracking prey, Santa watched for places that drew low-income workers. He found them at the train station, the bus station, bus stops and other places.

A cleaning lady burst into tears when Santa gave her $100. Santa spotted a young couple preparing to board a train and rushed to push money into the young man's hand. Later, in another neighborhood, Santa ducked into a small store and awarded each employee a Ben Franklin. As he came back out, a store manager followed.

"Hey!" the manager exclaimed. "You missed someone."

Santa handed some bills to Larry and sent him inside. The missed "worker" actually was a homeless man who agreed to help stock shelves for the opportunity to stay inside, away from the winter chill.

"We'd like you to have a very Merry Christmas," Larry said, handing him $200. The man's mouth fell open.

"Thank you, thank you," he said.

Back outside, the escorts were having such a good time they invited others by radio to join them. As darkness fell, Santa noticed that the number of patrol cars following him had grown to five or six. He chuckled. Oh, my, what a story this would be to tell his wife and children. An officer on bicycle tagged along, too.

The officers stayed back and let Santa work. He dished out cash quickly, told people "Merry Christmas" and moved to the next target. When some recipients asked if the money was real, the officers nodded.

Later, Larry spotted a drug store and pulled the van along the curb. The doors popped open. Santa and the others jumped out.

Pop. Pop. Pop.

An officer grabbed Santa, nearly lifting him off the ground, and shoved him back into the van. Still in the driver's seat, Larry ducked. He instantly knew the gunfire was close. Officers yelled for everyone to stay in the van while they checked it out.

The shots had been fired down the block, near the corner. Larry and Santa waited a few minutes before hearing that everything was okay. Maybe having the extra security was a good idea after all, Santa thought. His heart raced.

The next morning, Mike met up with Santa and Larry and other law enforcement officials at a Montgomery County police precinct. Mike noticed that Santa wore a black baseball cap bearing the names of the 10 people the snipers killed. Santa gave a second cap, just like his, to Mike.

Other donors already had helped victims' families in Montgomery County. Santa explained that he would give money to people who endured the terror because they lived or worked in the areas hit. Mike quietly wondered how Santa would find needy people in Montgomery County, the nation's sixth wealthiest county.

But Santa knew how. He avoided ritzy shopping districts and fancy restaurants and headed instead for a Salvation Army thrift store and other places frequented by minimum-wage workers, the homeless and unemployed.

He stuffed money into their hands before they realized what was happening. Several recipients stood dumbfounded, staring at the money like it carried bad germs. Some thought for sure the bills were fake, but then they saw the officers with Santa and recognized Montgomery County police Captain Nancy Demmi from television coverage of the sniper shootings. Then they knew the money was real and theirs to keep.

"You don't know how much this means to me," one recipient said. Some said they had been unable to purchase Christmas gifts. One man had promised his son shoes but didn't know how he was going to afford them. Another needed money for groceries. More than one had bills to pay. One man wanted to refill a prescription.

At a grocery store checkout counter, Santa noticed a scruffy man clutching a brownie. The locals knew him as "Minister Harry." He lived under a bridge. Santa slid him $100.

"Merry Christmas," Santa whispered. "Don't lose it."

Harry said something back. *Kansas City Star* reporter Matt Stearns, who was based in the paper's Washington office, moved closer and asked Harry what he had said.

"I told him, 'Don't worry, I won't lose it,'" Harry said. He looked at the bill. "I didn't think it would be this cold today. Now I can ride the bus all day."

As they moved around the county, Mike and Nancy gave a tour of the shooting sites, explaining what they publicly could about how the investigation unfolded.

John Allen Muhammad and John Lee Malvo allegedly had killed six persons in Montgomery County, including the first in their sadistic spree: a 55-year-old program analyst from Silver Spring. The county's other victims had been 39, 54, 34, 25 and 35 years old — a landscaper, a cab driver, a housekeeper, a nanny and a bus driver.

When shot, they had been buying groceries, mowing grass, getting gas, sitting on a bench, cleaning a van at a service station or driving a bus — just ordinary chores on what should have been ordinary fall days.

Terror permeated the area as the snipers remained loose, Mike and Nancy said. People feared they'd be next. Some stayed shuttered at home. Many fretted for their children, their family and their friends.

As Santa stood where victims had been shot and moved to where the shooters had positioned themselves for the ambush, he felt an eerie feeling — as if the presence of evil still resided there. He also felt sorrow for the victims' families. These people had died in an instant with no warning, and their lives had been stolen by someone they'd never harmed. A chill ran down his spine. He felt the hair on his arms and back raise.

Near a gas station where one shooting occurred, Santa handed $100 to each of five people waiting at a bus stop then went inside to give gas station employees money. When he came back out, the people at the bus stop were still hugging each other.

"Thank you, Santa!" one yelled.

One woman said she needed money to buy her disabled son Christmas gifts. She gushed over and over how Santa's gift would make Christmas possible.

Later, the group stopped for lunch at a small cafeteria and grabbed a table in the back, where Santa told stories about how he got started and why the bills he was handing out were stamped with the name "Ted Horn."

In the afternoon, they headed for Prince George County, where it was even easier to find needy people. The snipers wounded one person there, a 13-year-old boy shot as he walked to his middle school. Next, Santa visited Fairfax County, Virginia, and saw where FBI analyst Linda Franklin was killed while loading purchases into her car outside a Home Depot.

Santa listened as his new security crew explained how the shooting unfolded. The joyous mood that encompassed them as Santa gave away money faded to somberness as they recalled what happened.

Later, Santa handed out more money. Happiness returned. Larry, who was accompanying Santa for the first time, felt awed by how contagious his generosity became.

"That joy of seeing people react is infectious," he said later. "Everybody enjoys it."

Weeks later, long after Santa had gone home, the images of his visit remained fresh in Mike's mind.

"It was one of those things you remember your whole life," he said. "The reaction was the best part. There was that shock, that amazement, that disbelief."

Secret Santa seemed to have a knack for finding the right people, Mike said.

"This is probably something everybody fantasizes about — being able to go out and help people," he said. "It was a tremendously uplifting, positive experience."

Twenty-four

Return to Town Topic

Back in Kansas City later that month, Santa again rounded up his elves and hit the streets. During one hectic day handing out money, he ducked into Town Topic and scanned the worker's faces. None looked familiar.

"Where's Bonnie?" he asked.

"She's not here today," another employee said.

"Oh," Santa said, disappointed. "Okay then."

He left. The door jingled behind him.

A year earlier, after Bonnie bought the boots for her husband, Tom, he wore them every day until the cancer attacked his spine and he no longer could walk. The final two months of his life, Bonnie took a leave from work to care for him. When Tom died in August, she buried him in those boots.

Burdened with unpaid medical bills and the heavy heart of a widow who'd outlived two husbands, Bonnie returned to Town Topic. Returning was like, well, like returning to family. She started working for the small chain when she was 15 by lying about her age to get the job.

The day after Santa missed finding her there, Bonnie arrived for her usual day shift. About noon, a hunched man leaning on a cane and wearing an eye patch entered and took a seat in front of her. He ordered two hamburgers and coffee. Stubble grew on his chin. A fisherman's hat covered his white hair.

As the hunched man nursed his coffee after finishing his meal, one of Santa's elves entered carrying an envelope. He asked for Bonnie.

"This is from Secret Santa," Sheriff Tom said.

Bonnie tried to turn it away, but Sheriff Tom insisted she take it. She ducked into the back room and opened the envelope. Inside was $1,000, all in hundred-dollar bills.

When Bonnie returned to the front counter minutes later, she was crying. The hunched man noticed and nearly cried himself. He turned away so she wouldn't see his moist eyes.

He scribbled a note on a napkin, paid his bill and handed the note to another customer. "Will you give this to her after I leave?" the man asked, pointing at Bonnie.

The customer nodded.

A minute later, the customer got Bonnie's attention. "That man wanted you to have this," the customer said.

Bonnie took the napkin. The note was unsigned, but she knew who had written it.

I'm glad your husband got the boots. I hope this money will help you.

Bonnie sobbed so hard she lost her voice.

An hour later, a reporter called and asked what had happened. Bonnie's voice shook again. She didn't even realize Secret Santa had been sitting in front of her, she said. She wished she had given him a hug.

"He gave me too much money," she said between new sobs. "I didn't even know who it was until after he left. He wrote me a note.… This is so hard."

She still owed $3,000 in medical bills from Tom's treatments, she said. Maybe she'd use the money toward that. She thanked Santa.

"He truly is my angel from heaven," she said.

That evening, Secret Santa called Bonnie at her home to wish her a Merry Christmas. He didn't give a name, but there was no need.

Something he said about helping others made Bonnie rethink how she was going to use his latest gift. Every year that she could afford it, Bonnie liked to help a needy family for Christmas. Often, she provided a meal and some gifts. This year, she decided to divide Santa's gift into several envelopes and leave money in the homes of needy families. Twenty dollars here. Fifty dollars there. She knew just who she'd visit.

"He gave to us in secret," Bonnie explained later, "so I gave mine to everybody in secret. I can't do what he does, but I can give to others. I spread it out, which gives me great joy. I love to help people."

Twenty-five

'Put your hands up!'

D ecember weather in the Kansas City area can be fickle. Sometimes, it feels as warm as late summer or early fall. Other times, water lines inside homes freeze and break from bitter cold that seeps through walls and insulation. This Christmas Eve 2002 day, pouring rain washed the area, splashing off cars and dousing dormant yards.

Driving alone in Blue Springs, Santa saw a hitchhiker walking the outer road near eastbound Interstate 70. Santa felt sorry for him, especially because of the rain. He pulled over and offered the man a lift.

The hitchhiker said he wanted to get home to Memphis for Christmas. Knowing more than a little about Memphis, Santa grilled him on landmarks and other details. The hitchhiker answered correctly, which assured Santa the man wasn't fibbing.

Santa offered to pay for a motel room for the night and a bus ticket for the man to get home. Santa drove a little way east and turned into a hotel parking lot.

Inside the lobby, Santa told a manager he wanted to pay for a room for the drenched man. The manager seemed suspicious, so Santa showed him his deputy badge — a courtesy badge provided by the sheriff. Santa sometimes wore it so people wouldn't be afraid to take his money.

"I'm Deputy Bubba," Santa said, assuring the manager everything was okay.

As his clerk worked on the transaction, the manager stepped into another room and called the Jackson County Sheriff's Department.

"Do you have a Deputy Bubba?" he asked a captain.

"No," the captain answered. "We don't."

The manager dialed 911 and told Blue Springs police that someone in his lobby was impersonating an officer.

Santa finished paying for the hitchhiker's room and chatted a bit before heading outside. He had taken only a few steps when an authoritative voice stopped him in his tracks.

"Put your hands up," the person said. "Keep them up where I can see them."

Santa raised his hands slowly and looked around.

Police officers surrounded him. They wanted to know what he was doing.

"Call the sheriff," Santa pleaded.

"We already have," an officer responded.

"No," Santa said. "Call *the* sheriff."

Soon, Sheriff Tom's cell phone rang. A police dispatcher said Santa's real name and asked if Sheriff Tom knew him. Tom chuckled.

"What has he done now?" he asked.

The dispatcher paused.

"Is he Secret Santa?"

Not wanting to blow Santa's cover, Tom hesitated. "He works for him," he said, hedging.

The officers escorted Santa back inside the motel. The sheepish clerk pointed to the equally sheepish manager hiding in a corner and said, "He did it."

Later, Sheriff Tom called Santa to check on him.

"Need a bail bondsman?" Tom joked.

Santa laughed, but Tom had another, more serious message: Be careful about picking up strangers.

"You're grounded," he said.

Later, Tom recounted the story for friends.

"They were going to arrest Santa on Christmas Eve," he said. "Can you imagine?"

Twenty-six
Saving a life

Anewly arrived e-mail surprised Santa in late February 2003. A woman named Tina had written and attached a color photo of her husband standing behind her. His arms wrapped her in a warm embrace.

I wanted to take a moment to thank you, her note began.

She explained that God must have blessed Santa in a very special way because she had never known someone so unselfish and kind. She said that she had fallen on hard times before Santa helped her.

Santa leaned forward in his chair. He helped her?

The e-mail continued: *You had visited the homeless shelter where my family was at, and left money in our room. I always wanted to thank you for your kindness but have never been able to do so.*

What homeless shelter? How long ago? Santa couldn't remember meeting anyone named Tina at a homeless shelter. He studied the picture and shook his head. Her face didn't ring any bells.

Her family was doing better and had bought a used van, the e-mail said. She hoped they could buy license tags soon. She and her husband had moved into a Lee's Summit apartment. For once, she could breathe a sigh of relief.

A lot has happened to me over the last year. I lost my father and my sister was murdered on December 9, and every time I want to give up, I try to think of all the good things that happened the year you rescued me! And I say that, because the day you left the money, I set out to kill myself, and God had other plans in mind.

Wait a minute. She had planned to kill herself?

Santa leaned back and thought some more, but he still couldn't

143

place Tina or the homeless shelter. There were four or five shelters in Jackson County.

The e-mail concluded: *I can say this: Angels do live on earth and you are one of them. Thank you so much for everything!*

Santa answered and thanked Tina for writing. He sought more details, too. Two days later, she replied. She had received his gift during the Christmas season of 2001, while her family stayed at the Salvation Army Crossroads shelter in Independence.

Still unsure of the event, Santa called Sheriff Tom and asked whether he remembered it.

He did. After a day of giving out money, Santa had handed leftover cash to Tom and said, "Here, give this to your favorite charity." Later, Sheriff Tom gave $200 to a homeless man he saw near a street. He took the rest to Crossroads and placed it on a family's dresser.

Ah-ha! Mystery solved.

Santa had received more than a thousand e-mails since 2001, but none matched this one. And this time, Sheriff Tom had helped save a life.

Twenty-seven
After the wildfires

Steven and Pam Samson looked perplexed when several strangers piled out of a white van and walked uphill toward the scenic ridge where their Southern California home once stood — before the wildfire consumed it.

"We're here from Missouri," said one of the strangers, a plump man in a red T-shirt. "Where was your house?"

"Man, you're standing on it," answered Steven Samson, by then a trailer dweller.

The stranger pulled three crisp hundred-dollar bills from his pocket and thrust them toward Samson.

"It's to use for Christmas or whatever," Santa said. "Hope it helps."

Tears welled in Samson's eyes. A union member, he hadn't worked in weeks because of a grocer strike in San Diego County. His mortgage company was threatening foreclosure on a house that no longer existed. The cable company demanded payment on service no longer provided.

Samson faced other bills, too, and he wanted to replace Christmas gifts, which his wife had bought early while on sale. The gifts perished along with their 900-square-foot home when the wildfire consumed it in late October.

Santa turned to Samson's wife, Pam, and offered another $300. She waved it off.

"You've helped enough," she said.

Santa persisted. She relented.

"Oh, wow," Steven Samson said softly. "This is too much. Thank you, thank you."

Two months earlier, deep in the dry California timber, a lost hunter decided rescuers would find him easier if he set a signal fire. It was a bad decision. Though the hunter lived, he ignited a fast-moving blaze that ate up 200 acres a minute the first 24 hours alone. That's a square mile every three minutes. It was as if someone had pointed a giant blowtorch on the hills east of San Diego.

The wildfire blackened 280,278 acres, destroyed about 2,400 homes and killed 14 persons in San Diego County in the fall of 2003. Known as the Cedar fire — the largest wildfire in California history — it was one of 11 wildfires that scorched Southern California that year. Authorities designated five counties as federal disaster areas.

Watching the news back in Missouri that fall, Santa saw an interview with a victim who had lost both his job and his house, just like Steven Samson.

Man! That's a double dose of pain, Santa thought.

He decided to visit California in December. He invited fire Captain Ray Wynn, by now a veteran elf, and recruited a relative rookie: Carl Tripp, a battalion chief who worked with Ray. Both had watched Santa give the first Tvedten Angel award.

They flew to San Diego days before Christmas and checked into a downtown hotel, where they met up with another rookie elf: legendary Chicago Bears linebacker Dick Butkus, who brought a friend from Malibu. Retired FBI agent Larry McCormick flew in from Arizona to serve as the group's driver.

Near their high-rise hotel, foot traffic bustled on busy neighboring streets, especially along blocks teeming with restaurants. Here, the city looked normal. Smoke that choked the region two months earlier had vanished.

Yet on the east edge of town, blackened fields lapped both shoulders of highways, reminding residents and visitors alike of the fire's furry. Incredibly, the blaze had jumped eight lanes or more in spots, shutting down busy interstates for hours.

Up the hills to the east, vast stretches of timber and tall shrubs no longer existed, replaced by a barren landscape that threatened to slip and slide when heavy rains arrived. Much of the cinnamon-and-soot-colored terrain looked more like it belonged on the moon or Mars than Earth.

Though insurance covered about a third of victims, others were uninsured or underinsured. Many didn't know how they would rebuild. The usual groups — federal agencies, charities, volunteers — came to help. But so did scam artists, who overcharged the uninformed.

Mike Vogt, a fire battalion chief in the town of Ramona, and deputies with the San Diego County Sheriff's Department escorted Santa through charred rural canyons and some of the area's hard-hit small towns. They bypassed high-income neighborhoods, where residents most likely had insurance.

Much like a Midwestern tornado, the fire skipped some structures while obliterating others. Some of the heaviest-hit communities lost half their homes.

One of Santa's first stops was Harbison Canyon, about 28 miles east of downtown San Diego. Bracketed by the hills, the canyon's shape funneled the fire straight through town, where it burned 288 homes. Despite orders to stay away, some homeowners rushed back afterward to defend what was left from opportunistic and insensitive looters.

When Santa arrived on a December weekday, the canyon sat largely deserted. Larry parked the van near a disaster recovery center. Santa strolled inside. Only a few people were there, mostly volunteers preparing donated furniture for distribution. One worker agreed to lead Santa's group on a town tour.

Block after block, Santa walked past charred structures, house-less foundations, temporary tents and Federal Emergency Management Agency trailers. He spotted a 37-year-old man working in his yard and stopped to chat. The man motioned to a temporary trailer nearby and said his 73-year-old mother was inside. The fire destroyed their house. Santa handed him $200.

"God bless you," the man said. "Mom will be pleased."

Down the road, the foundations of two destroyed houses flanked a house that survived.

"Look," Santa said, pointing to the house. "Golly, that's amazing."

Around a bend, Santa and his elves happened upon a group of eight friends chatting in lawn chairs near temporary trailers. Many wore short sleeves as they basked in the sun.

"Howdy folks," Santa said. "How y'all doing?"

He handed each person $100, part of the $25,000 he brought.

Montie Roberts, who lost his restaurant and bar, shook his head. "This is awful nice," he said. "It's fantastic."

From there, Santa's caravan drove three miles east to Crest, a village of about 1,100 homes. The fire consumed 280 of them, including the Samsons' house.

A sign in the window of Crest's undamaged fire station announced that the East County Fire Department was collecting Christmas toys for fire victims. Larry pulled the van into the parking lot. Chief Darrell Jobes came outside with a volunteer. He hesitated when he saw one of Santa's elves.

"Is that Dick Butkus from football?" Jobes asked.

Santa nodded.

"It's a pleasure to meet you," Jobes said, grinning as he held out his hand for Dick.

Santa counted $1,000 for relief efforts and handed it to Challais McDonald, a volunteer who was helping organize the toy drive. Her eyes widened.

"You flew down here to do this?" she asked. "Thank you!"

Sheriff's deputies escorted Santa to a ridge where residents evacuated down the only available road. Behind them, the blaze blocked the other route out of town. Traffic stretched bumper-to-bumper, jammed as badly as a city highway during rush hour. When the fire crested the hill, many saw it in their rearview mirrors. Heat licked the last evacuees.

"I was only scared once during that fire," a deputy told Santa, "and that was it."

The last in line, a sheriff's deputy, barely escaped, he said. Heat seared the star emblem on the car's door.

The Samsons lived in their Crest home 22 years, raising two children there. When Santa visited, only a concrete slab remained.

Finding fire victims proved more difficult than Santa had expected. Lot after charred lot sat empty, with no owners in sight. Some people had relocated. Others lived in trailers on their old lots, but many of them were away at work.

In El Cajon, a city at the base of the hills, Santa spotted a 35-year-old woman selling flowers. Larry parked the van.

"Do we get a discount if we buy them in bulk?" Ray asked the woman.

"It's $185 for all of these," Kathy Peters said, waving her hand over the fresh-cut bouquets.

"All right," Santa said in a voice that sounded disappointed, as if the price were too high. "You drive a hard bargain. Here's $300."

Kathy looked at Santa as if he were crazy.

"All right, we'll give you $400," Santa said. "We are from Missouri and we like pretty flowers."

Kathy stared at him, still speechless.

"I tell you what," Santa said. "I don't have any place to put these. Let me see. …"

He gave her the flowers back, told her to keep the money and suggested she try selling the flowers again.

"That's a Christmas present from us," Santa said. "Merry Christmas."

And he dashed away.

"Whoa," Kathy said. "What a shock. I never had anything like that happen to me before."

Though not a fire victim, she needed the money. She had purchased each of her children, ages 18, 15 and 12, one gift apiece for Christmas. Now, it would be a nicer Christmas.

The next day, Santa's crew hit the highway to visit other towns.

Outside Ramona, deputies mentioned that a tiny neighborhood called Fernbank suffered heavily. They took Santa down a winding road to where several of the families previously lived in the timber.

One family had insurance and planned to rebuild. A second was underinsured and needed help. A third had no insurance and sought assistance from churches and charities, as well as federal officials.

The deputies had a special couple in mind along this road. They directed Santa toward a FEMA trailer parked near charred ruins of a small house. This was where Carmen and Laman Sadler, who had been married 50 years, lost their home of 27 years. Though age had slowed them, Laman still called his wife "Lightning."

One day earlier, while gently stirring through debris with the tip of her cane, Carmen had uncovered the cracked cover of a ceramic butter dish — one of their wedding gifts. The bottom was gone, like the rest of their belongings.

Habitat for Humanity had promised to help them rebuild, once funds could be raised.

When Santa arrived, the Sadlers came outside of their one-bedroom trailer and smiled, pleased to have visitors.

"What did you do when you heard the fire was coming?" Santa asked.

"Friends called us at 3:30 on a Sunday morning and told us it wasn't looking good," Laman began. "We seen fire coming over the mountain. I started putting stuff in the car."

The fire consumed their rose garden, grape arbor, pictures, albums, books and everything else. They saved only what fit in their aging car that hurried morning.

"A few clothes was about it," Laman said.

"How are you doing right now?" Santa asked.

"We have an upbeat attitude," Carmen said.

Santa had not planned it, but he suddenly decided to name the Sadlers honorary Tvedten Angels. Santa explained the award to the Sadlers, who listened quietly.

"With that comes an honorarium in his name," Santa said. "One thousand dollars."

Tears formed in Carmen's eyes.

"Thank you," Laman said before also beginning to cry. He handed his wife a tissue. Both wiped away tears.

"You all are so wonderful," Laman said. "Everybody has been so kind."

Less than a half-mile away, Santa stopped at a fenced property where a large sign proclaimed: "Single mom with six kids. Lost it all. Need help."

Santa sneaked through a fence opening to where three mailboxes lay on the ground. He put $700 in the middle box, one bill for each child and one for the mother, Wanda Kwiatt. Insurance covered only about one-fifth of their loss.

Sheriff's Deputy Bill Brecheisen reached Wanda on a cell phone and handed it to Santa.

"Hello?" Santa said. "Who am I talking to? Wanda?"

He paused.

"Just say I'm Secret Santa," he said. "We are from Kansas City.… We left you a Christmas present for you and your six children."

He told her where to find the money and said, "We hope it helps out a little bit this Christmas."

Wanda said she would let her "kiddos" buy gifts for each other.

Santa handed the phone to a *Kansas City Star* reporter.

"There will be some happy shoppers," Wanda told the reporter, who stood in the middle of the road trying to maintain a signal. Deputies motioned for two oncoming cars to wait while the reporter talked. "Tell him he will make Christmas for us. God bless him," Wanda added.

Later in nearby Ramona, Santa walked along the main street, looking for people to help. He found Hennie Volschen, who asked: "Is this real? Is it the real green thing? My gosh."

Santa noticed a man aboard a road grader waiting at a light. Santa turned to two deputies and suggested they flag down the man and give him money. Santa handed $100 to one deputy. They trotted to their car, flipped on their lights and pulled behind the grader. At first, the driver plodded ahead, trailed by the slow-moving sheriff's car. Some elves and two photographers chased on foot.

After stopping about block away, the perplexed driver turned to a deputy and asked, "What do you want?"

Having watched Santa's playful tricks, the deputy coined one of his own. He asked the driver for proof of registration. The driver looked puzzled. Since when did he need registration for a road grader?

The deputy grinned, held out the hundred-dollar bill and said, "Santa Claus said you should go buy some registration for it."

The deputies turned back to where Santa waited. He laughed. They laughed, too.

After lunch, the group headed east to Julian, a Cuyamaca mountain town known for its apple pies, gold rush heritage and retreat-like setting among oak and pine trees. Though imperiled by the fires, the town's historic Main Street survived.

At a volunteer fire department station, Santa learned that seven firefighters lost their homes. Santa asked a firefighter if he had two department ball caps he would be willing to sell. If so, Santa would pay him $1,000 apiece.

"I'll give you my wife's hat for that," one eager firefighter said.

Soon, Santa had two caps.

The group stopped for pies at Mom's, one of the town's historic eateries. Afterward, Santa gave each employee a Ben Franklin.

"This is the best day of my life," said one, who earned $6.75 an hour.

Santa headed outside to the sidewalk, where he dropped a hundred-dollar bill and watched to see who would pick it up. Four people passed. None stopped.

"I wish I could say it was mine," one man said.

Santa shook his head and retrieved the bill.

At a disaster relief center, Santa gave several people money. The recipients thanked him with hugs.

As he's prone to do in Missouri, Santa also searched for thrift stores and self-service laundries. While looking, he spotted a woman filling the radiator of a battered 1975 Chevy truck near a gas station. "Stop the van," Santa said. He jumped out and slipped her $100. She cried. He gave her $200 more. She cried harder. A part-time Walgreens employee, Becky Hernandez had received a $253.76 paycheck earlier in the day and already spent it.

"I'm totally overwhelmed," the 40-year-old mother said. "Stuff like this I never thought existed.... May the Lord watch him always. He will be in my thoughts and prayers for the rest of my days."

The deputies soon found a thrift store. Santa handed Dick several bills and told his 6-foot-3 elf to get busy. Dick, new to this type of philanthropy, gingerly approached two men in the shoe aisle.

"Here," he said, handing over one bill. "Use this to pay for your shoes."

"What's going on here?" Greg Coon of La Mesa asked. Told by reporters that he had just been given money from a former NFL player, he and his friend shrugged.

"We're not football fans," the friend said.

In another aisle, parents of seven children searched for clothing. One daughter spotted a dress she liked. It cost $10. The girl's mom shook her head. That was too much.

Dick handed the family $300. The mom hugged him.

"It's a blessing," said Roxanne Hernandez, who along with her husband was unemployed. "This means I can buy my kids clothes and Christmas presents."

At a laundry, Santa offered money to a woman who shook her head and refused. She suspected a scam. Another woman accepted and asked who Santa was.

"He's from Kansas City," someone answered.

"No," she said. "He's from the North Pole."

Later, Santa spotted a Salvation Army banner hanging on a shopping center. The site had been set up to collect toy and food donations. Right now, it was closed. Volunteers inside were wrapping up for the day.

Santa and some elves sneaked in through an unlocked door. Major Glen Madsen demanded to know who everyone was and what they wanted. Ray and Carl stepped forwarded and shook his hand.

"We're from Kansas City," one said.

Madsen looked nervous.

"We're closed now," he said.

Santa reached into a pocket. "We brought you $500," he said.

"You're freaking me out, guys," Major Madsen answered, looking even more nervous. "Come on, now. What's going on here?"

"I'm a friend of the Army," Santa said. He handed his donation to Major Madsen and left the way he had entered.

"I'm just absolutely flabbergasted," Major Madsen said.

A reporter explained that the donor was known as Secret Santa in Kansas City. Major Madsen raised his eyebrows. He raced to the parking lot.

"Secret Santa!" he hollered. "You freaked me out. I thought the FBI was coming after me or something."

Elves sitting in the van laughed.

Santa's driver was a retired FBI agent.

Twenty-eight
'I didn't believe'

Any given year, in the days leading up to Christmas, a few gallons of gasoline can cost Santa $100 or more, no matter what the price-per-gallon sign says.

At one Kansas City station in December 2003, he darted inside the small convenience store where a lone clerk worked behind a counter. Santa picked up two bottles of water and offered a Ben Franklin in trade.

"Look!" the surprised clerk said as he showed his next customers the cash.

Outside, Santa paused. Forty-five-year-old Geneva Fields sat at a gas pump in a battered 14-year-old car. The driver's window was rolled down. Santa walked up, reached in and offered Geneva $100.

"Ma'am, this is for you," he said.

"No!" she exclaimed. "No! God, no! You've got to be kidding. Is it real? Can I hug you?"

Santa chuckled.

"Say a prayer for me," he said. "I can always use some of those."

He dipped a hand back into a pocket.

"I got another one for you," Santa said before dashing off, leaving two photographers and a reporter staring at Geneva.

Tears poured, leaving streaks on her plump cheeks.

"No! No! Oh, God!" she squealed. "This can't be real."

She started another sentence, but a sob interrupted it. She took a deep breath and started again.

"Tell him I said, 'Thank you so very much.'"

She wiped her cheeks.

"Oh, God. This ain't real. Not me. This ain't real."

A mother of three and grandmother of three, she needed money for Christmas gifts. Plus, she'd only quenched a little of her gas tank's thirst. Now, she could pump more gas into the car.

"I heard about him," she said of Santa, "but I didn't believe."

§ § §

Santa feared if he returned to Town Topic a third year in a row, someone inside might recognize him. So he sent an elf instead.

The elf gave each employee, including Bonnie, $100.

"You've got to admit, he's pretty slick," Bonnie said later. "To be able to bless people like that, that's just awesome."

She often wonders who Secret Santa is.

"I don't have a clue," she said. "Not a clue."

Twenty-nine

A new home

Tracy Brazelton reported to work inside a Kansas City shopping mall a few days before Christmas 2003 uncertain what her future held.

A single mother attending nursing school while raising three girls, she found it impossible to make her house payments. Her house of four years was to be sold on the Clay County courthouse steps in a few weeks. She and her daughters, ages 11, 9 and 5, needed another place to live.

Convinced they were about to become homeless, one of her daughters had asked for a sleeping bag for Christmas. Mom hugged her girls and told them everything would be okay as long as they were together.

One recent Sunday, Tracy had told her story at a Catholic church. Sitting in the audience, Kansas City firefighter Patrick Shea and his wife, Suellen, looked at each other. Both wanted to help. Suellen, who was a nurse, asked her husband afterward what they could do. He called another firefighter, who contacted Secret Santa.

When he heard Tracy's story, Santa's heart melted. Sure, he wanted to help, but how? A few Ben Franklins wouldn't solve anything.

Three days before Christmas, he called Tracy and promised to help her find a house.

"What is your name?" she asked.

"That's not important," he answered.

He told her not to worry and to have faith in God.

The next day, Santa pulled into the parking lot of the mall where Tracy worked. A few elves, two reporters and two photographers joined him. Though little time remained before Christmas, the mall appeared in a mid-week slumber. Few shoppers had arrived that frigid morning.

Sheriff Tom walked ahead and peeked into the children's clothing store where Tracy worked. Three employees straightened clothes in preparation for the rush to come. None wore a name tag. Sheriff Tom spotted a mall security officer and asked if he knew which one was Tracy.

Sheriff Tom returned to where Santa waited.

"Tracy is the one in the pink sweater," he reported.

Elves and journalists sauntered into the store and pretended to browse. Santa followed a minute later wearing a fake white beard and a red Santa hat.

He walked straight to his target.

"Tracy?"

"Yes."

The others converged on Tracy and Santa.

"Merry Christmas," Santa said. "We are all here from the fire department, and we've got something special for you."

Santa held up a certificate, which named her "Mom of the Year" for displaying the courage, determination and willingness to help others in light of difficult circumstances. Santa had named her a John Tvedten Angel, too.

Tracy's chin quivered. A tear formed. She wiped her eye. Sheriff Tom moved closer and handed her $5,000 for the children.

"Merry Christmas from Santa and all of his elves," Sheriff Tom said.

Santa reminded Tracy of his promise to help her find a house. The money was in addition to that promise, he told her.

New tears ran in lines down her cheeks. She hugged an elf.

"I don't know what to say," she told Santa, her voice shaking. "Thank you is not enough."

Santa turned to leave. Tracy continued to cry.

"I didn't know how many people cared," she said through the

tears.

Three weeks later, on a Saturday, about 15 off-duty firefighters arrived at Tracy's home with pickup trucks and a moving van. One of them wore a full-fledged Santa suit made by his mother. Secret Santa arrived in street clothes.

Tracy had found a home to rent with a spacious back yard her girls loved. She had called Santa, who had called the landlord and said that he would pay six months' rent if the landlord would provide one month for free. It was a deal.

Patrick recruited co-workers from his fire station to help. Ray Wynn recruited other volunteers from his station.

"All we had to do was mention it," Patrick said. "These guys are great."

Tracy already had packed her belongings in boxes marked according to the room they were destined for at the new house. Sidestepping a cat and plants, the firefighters carted the boxes from the split-level house to the trucks.

"I picture firefighters going to fires to rescue people," Tracy said. "I guess they do rescues all the time."

Someone asked what all the help meant to her.

"I've come to realize that home is where the heart is, and my heart is with my children," she said. "They'll take us to a new home, and my heart will be there because it's with my kids."

With the moving van and trucks full, and the house nearly empty, the volunteer drivers started their engines. A caravan jogged through neighborhoods until reaching Tracy's new abode. Inside, 5-year-old Sidney Brazelton motioned Santa to follow her on a tour. She raced through the house, pointing out the three bedrooms upstairs before scampering downstairs to show off a carpeted play area and a big closet.

"Isn't this great?" she asked, beaming.

Santa nodded.

"Yes it is."

The firefighters unloaded the trucks. Once again, it took an hour.

After finishing, they asked if Tracy needed anything else.

Santa already had decided that she did need something. Standing in her living room, he pulled out his cell phone and dialed a friend. "I need a favor," he said. After a few minutes, Santa hung up and turned to Tracy to announce a surprise: Bob Teel, the president of a local security company, had agreed to install a home security system. For free.

Tracy looked stunned.

"Okay," she said softly. "Tell your friend I said thank you."

The firefighters gathered outside for a group picture before departing. As Tracy watched them go, gratitude washed over her.

"Give them my heartfelt thanks," she told one of the last to leave. "Thank you, thank you, thank you so much."

Thirty

Florida's hurricanes

When her captain called her into his Florida office and said, "Close the door," Desoto County Deputy Sheriff Maria Trevino feared she'd done something wrong.

Instead, her boss dangled a special assignment: provide security for Secret Santa, a stranger coming to Florida to help hurricane victims and the poor.

Her captain didn't know Santa. Someone up the line had called him. This Santa, the captain had been told, already had visited Ground Zero in 2001 and spread money through San Diego County in California following devastating wild fires in 2003.

"Nobody knows who he is," the captain told Maria. "Do you want to spend some time with him?"

Maria hesitated.

"Are you sure this guy is legitimate?" she asked.

§ § §

Earlier in the year, Santa considered not making any long distance trips during his 2004 holiday giving period. He pondered simply staying on his home turf.

But weeks after an unprecedented four hurricanes tossed Florida around — tearing thousands of roofs, shredding citrus groves and devastating the tourism industry — Santa changed his mind. The hurricanes struck over 42 days, killed 117, destroyed more than 25,000 homes and heavily damaged tens of thousands of other build-

ings. Damage estimates exceeded $42 billion in Florida alone.
Santa began mapping plans in November.

"Christmas time is a time people are supposed to be happy — it's supposed to be a time of giving," Santa said. "I think this is an opportunity to show in a small way what Christ would tell us to do."

With "elves" making the security arrangements and helping with other details, Santa booked a flight to Tampa and targeted areas to the south, including Port Charlotte and Punta Gorda, neighboring towns devastated by Hurricane Charley, the first and fiercest of the four storms.

The trip turned into something more, however, when cancer took the life of one of Santa's good friends in southern Florida the Monday after Thanksgiving.

The friend, Charlie Meyerson, died at home two weeks shy of his 89th birthday. A former New York bookmaker, he'd been a legendary casino host in Las Vegas. Some called him a "superhost" during his time at the Mirage. His obituary said he "touched thousands of lives and treasured his many friendships," which included a long relationship with casino developer Steve Wynn. He left his wife and eight children, nine grandchildren and four great-grandchildren.

Santa considered Charlie one of the most extraordinary individuals he'd ever met, a compassionate and generous human being. "He was the most loyal friend a person could ever hope for."

Years earlier, Santa and Charlie had been sharing breakfast at a golf event when Santa decided to tell Charlie the Secret Santa story. Until then, Charlie knew Santa only by Santa's real name.

Each succeeding year, Charlie longed to hear Santa's stories of giving away money at Christmas. At the end of those conversations, Charlie often would say, "Santa Claus, I just talked to God, and he's got a special place for you in heaven."

Santa would answer, "Charlie, God's got a special place for you as well."

So after Charlie's death, Santa knew he had to dedicate his 2004 Christmas season to Charlie. In addition to giving away money in

Florida, he'd fly to Las Vegas.

He withdrew a record $100,000 from the bank. Before heading to Florida with nearly a third of it, he paid for the creation of two ink stamps. One bore Charlie's name. The other bore Santa's web address: www.secretsantausa.com.

Santa hoped that anyone who received a bill, even if it came from a bank weeks after Santa had given it to someone else, would be intrigued enough to look up the website. There, Santa would explain Charlie's friendship and encourage recipients to write in and say where they'd gotten the Ben Franklin.

"This is one of the most special trips of all," Santa said as he prepared for Florida.

§ § §

Hurricane Charley intensified into a Category 4 storm just before slamming the Gulf Coast on August 13. It tore apart tourist hotspot Captiva Island and heavily damaged other islands before turning east into Charlotte Harbor and bearing down on Punta Gorda and Port Charlotte. Winds peeled roofs off fire stations and rolled mobile homes like dice. Metal power poles bent over as if trying to touch their toes then froze there.

The storm roared inland, too, battering places like Arcadia and Wauchula, poor migrant-worker communities.

Later, Hurricanes Frances and Jeanne thumped some of the same areas after arriving from the Atlantic Ocean. The fourth storm, Hurricane Ivan, dumped more rain on an already over-saturated state as it swirled north through the Gulf and slammed Florida's panhandle.

By December, blue tarps still covered 135,000 Florida roofs in a disaster area that stretched 750 miles. Thousands of victims remained homeless or lived in temporary residences, such as the 11,500 trailers provided by federal officials. Victims could stay in the trailers for 18 months, but some officials predicted that wouldn't be long enough. Complete recovery, they said, could take years.

In Charlotte County, the school district lost so many buildings, classes split into shifts for the 2004-2005 school year. Students living in a mobile home park set up by federal officials rode buses miles north to school.

The mobile home park — the largest of its kind in Florida — contained 350 homes by mid-December and prepared to add 200 more. Many people in the area, some living in cars, remained on waiting lists for housing. Others who earlier thought their homes were okay now were being forced out by mold, a growing problem.

Tampa avoided major damage when Charley turned east earlier than expected. Landing at the airport there gave Santa no indication of what awaited miles to the south.

A 45-foot-long, million-dollar luxury bus owned and driven by L.D. Stewart, the founder of Hooters restaurants, served as one of Santa's sleighs. Santa also rented a van, which made it easier to troll neighborhoods.

His elves included many veterans: a Kansas City firefighter, Jackson County's sheriff, a retired FBI agent and a former Chicago Bear.

L.D. and Dick Butkus played college football together. Decades later, they still enjoyed smoking cigars together, grilling hearty food and critiquing current NFL players. As L.D. drove his bus south, Dick sat in the front passenger seat and talked football. They questioned why some modern players wear long hair flowing out the back of their helmets.

"In our day," Dick said, "we grabbed any hair we could and pulled. We'd get in those piles (of players) and pull hard. Guys didn't let their hair get long for a reason."

Santa slid into a leather seat at one of the tables toward the back of the bus, just in front of the full-size refrigerator and the wall-mounted television. He laid three stacks of $10,000 each on the table then pulled out his special stamps and a pad of red ink.

"I'm going to personally stamp every one of these hundred-dollar bills," he said, "right by the In God we Trust."

He grabbed the Charlie Meyerson stamp and began.

164

§ § §

Further south, Deputy Maria wondered how Santa would choose his recipients. She thought about the many people she knew who could use a boost, including several crime victims she met through investigations. Maybe he'd give them money.

She opened a pocket-sized notepad and jotted a list.

§ § §

L.D. pulled the big bus into a Stop-N-Shop in Bowling Green, the northernmost town in Hardee County, population 28,000. More than 40 miles inland, it had suffered heavy damages.

Deputy Sylvia Estes and others from the Hardee County Sheriff's Department greeted the bus and, after introductions, escorted it south, to the Wal-Mart in Wauchula, a heavily migrant community. The hurricanes so riddled area housing, five or six migrant families at a time now shared mobile homes. Their jobs — picking ripe citrus — had been curtailed severely.

"This county lost 50 percent of its grapefruit crop and 30 to 40 percent of oranges and tangerines," explained Colonel Arnold Lanier, one of the officers providing security.

Santa needed batteries, so he walked toward the Wal-Mart entrance with Sheriff Tom while the others loitered in the outer edge of the parking lot. As he neared the front door, Santa spotted a man loading purchases into a taxi.

"I'm from Kansas City," Santa told the man and his wife.

"I was born in Kansas City, Missouri," Irene Reyna, 47, answered. "Jackson County."

Santa pointed to Tom.

"Guess what?" Santa said. "This gentleman is the sheriff of Jackson County."

"No way!" Reyna said. "I work for the sheriff here."

She beamed when Santa gave her a hundred-dollar bill. Her

husband received one, too. Santa smiled. How strange that the first person he decided to help had Kansas City roots.

Charley destroyed the couple's home. For three or four nights afterward, they slept in their car. Parents of nine children and grandparents of 24, they opened the taxi service after the hurricanes.

"We weren't planning to have Christmas," Reyna said. "Now we'll get what we can."

Leaving the big bus at Wal-Mart, Santa climbed into the smaller van and scouted for targets. He saw a transient named Roberto sorting through trash in a parking lot trash bin. Santa hopped out.

"I want you to have a Merry Christmas," Santa told Roberto as he slipped him a bill.

Later, Santa entered a busy laundry and paused to let his eyes adjust from the bright sunshine. Rows of washers and dryers whirled and groaned. The smell of bleach and detergent permeated the moisture-laden air. Dryer doors popped open and slammed shut, releasing spurts of warmth into the already warm room.

Santa offered quick greetings. "We, uh, want you to have a Merry Christmas," he told one woman. "That's for you."

"Is it real?" she asked in Spanish, a look of surprise on her face.

Another woman, who lost her home in the hurricane, tried to avoid Santa's offer.

"I can't take this," Yer Lee said, backing up and raising her hands.

"Then give it to your favorite charity," Santa said.

"Okay," she said hesitantly. "I'll give it to the church. Thank you."

In the next aisle, Santa spotted Calixto Patricio opening a front-loading washer to remove clothes. With a quick flick of his wrist, Santa stuck a folded bill in the lip inside the door. Calixto stared at the money and froze.

"Merry Christmas," Santa said. "That's for your family."

Calixto spoke no English.

"I don't want to take it," he said in Spanish to Deputy Sylvia, who was trailing Santa. "Are you sending me back to Mexico? No, I don't want it."

"It's for you to enjoy," Sylvia explained.

After more assurances, Calixto finally understood. He smiled.

"Tell him thank you," he said.

Dick noticed children toward the front of the laundry asking their parents for quarters. He and Ray pooled $100 and requested 400 quarters from the manager. Dick borrowed a small bucket to hold the coins then walked through the laundry, offering children a handful. One young girl used both hands to scoop up quarters. In less than a minute, the bucket emptied.

Everywhere Santa and his elves went, hurricane victims told similar stories. Charley took their roof. Or their porch. Or their home. Or soaked through their walls, drenching carpet and bedding and clothes. Now, they were sharing a trailer with friends or staying in a motel or looking for a new home.

They'd received food, clothing and in some cases housing assistance from the government. This stranger carrying hundred-dollar bills stunned them.

"I thought he was joking," said Maria Cleto, who planned to use her cash for Christmas gifts.

"I thought it was a trick at first," said Jim Patrick, co-owner of the laundry.

Juana Valadez, the mother of a 5-year-old child, said Santa came through at the right time.

"My husband just got laid off," she said. "Right now, I'm the only one working."

Santa and his elves headed back to Wal-Mart and grabbed a late lunch of pizza inside the bus. As they ate, Sheriff Tom spotted two women pushing shopping carts through the lot. Children surrounded them.

"I think you've got a target outside," Tom told Santa.

Santa bounded down the bus steps and struck up a conversation with Maria Calvillo, mother of seven children, ages 21, 17, 16, 14, 12, 9 and 3. She brought her youngest to Wal-Mart to let him ride the toy horse, she said. Her family still lived in their hurricane-damaged home, with its cracked ceiling, wet carpet and molded walls. Unaware that Charley approached, they weathered the storm huddled in the house.

Santa gave her $100 for each child, as much money as her husband could earn in seven days picking crops. They had no Christmas tree, no lights, she said.

"I'm still in shock," she said later. "I'm still nervous. I can't believe it. He's going to have a good Christmas. God is going to help him a lot for helping people."

§ § §

Rays from the afternoon sun began to lengthen as the caravan headed south again on U.S. 17, this time bound for neighboring Desoto County.

Deputy Maria watched them pull into the lot near her sheriff's department station. Santa and the elves scrambled out of the bus, eager to stretch their legs. Santa walked toward Maria. She opened her notebook and timidly showed him her list. A former school teacher, she had wanted for years to be a law enforcement officer. Now, after five years on the job, she put up with her daughter kidding her that she got too involved with victims. Her daughter caller her "Save the World." But Maria believed it was her duty to help.

So now, she saw an opportunity. Was Santa interested in helping these people?

Santa looked at her pad and smiled.

"We're going to get everybody on the list," he said. "Raise your right hand. You are now an official elf of Secret Santa."

They laughed and exchanged high fives.

Another deputy, Bryon Waters, escorted them in a patrol car while Maria rode in the van, explaining the stories of the families they would visit.

They knocked on the trailer door of a 74-year-old woman and her son, who had huddled in their car, praying that the winds wouldn't blow out their windshield, when Charley hit. Santa gave them $800.

"I can't take your money, sir," the woman's son, Johnny Garcia, said when Santa offered it. After Santa insisted, Johnny stared at the money before looking up at his benefactor. "I don't know what to say. I guess: God bless all of you guys. I ain't ever had nobody do this for us."

Later Maria and Santa searched for a man who'd been beaten and robbed of $50. When they found him, Santa gave him $300.

After dark, the van pulled onto the property of a husband, wife and son. Lights on a parked 10-year-old Chevy Tahoe clicked on. The three of them, unable to pay their electric bill, had hunkered down for the night in the Tahoe as the temperature dipped into the 50s. They wondered who was entering their driveway. Dad hopped out. So did his son, without a coat because he didn't own one. Santa chatted before giving them hotel money, bill money and gift money.

Santa headed to the countryside to visit Kenny Albritton, a sheriff's deputy who spent three years as a United Nations police officer in Kosovo. Charley had torn off his porch screen. Kenny was saving to buy a car, Maria told Santa en route, and he'd recently lost his mother.

When Kenny answered his door with his three-year-old daughter, Zhaneta, in his arms, he was surprised to see a crowd. Sheriff Tom said he had someone he wanted the family to meet: Santa Claus.

"We have an extensive database in Kansas City where we do sleigh rides," said Santa, who was wearing his trademark white coveralls and red flannel shirt. "The data is fed from the North Pole."

"Is that good or bad?" Kenny asked.

"It's a good thing," Santa said. "We came all the way from Kansas City to bring you a Christmas present."

He pulled out a hundred-dollar bill.

"Oh, wow," Kenny said.

Then Santa counted out $1,000. Kenny's wife, Merita, began to cry.

"I don't know what to say," Kenny said. "Thank you very much."

For several seconds, no one spoke. Santa shuffled his feet.

"Are you a football fan?" Santa asked. He pointed to Dick, who had been standing in the shadows. Kenny's eyes widened.

"Oh my God!" he exclaimed, offering his hand for a shake. "Mr. Butkus. Wow. It's nice to meet you."

Kenny sent his wife after a camera. The family posed with Dick.

From there, Santa dropped in on 92-year-old Frank Peterson, a toothless retiree who lived on Social Security and food stamps. Charley demolished his home. FEMA had provided a small trailer. Uninsured, he didn't know how he'd rebuild. Two weeks earlier, someone stole his wallet and $900, a crime Maria was trying to solve.

"This guy won my heart when I came out and did an investigation," Maria told Santa before they arrived.

Inside the cozy trailer, Santa delved into a speech.

"Well, Mr. Peterson," he said, "God has sent you an angel." He pointed to Maria. "She is an angel."

"I know," Frank answered as he looked at the deputy and called her name, dragging the syllables as he said it. "Ma-reeee-a."

Santa continued. "A very good man once told me: 'Santa Claus, I once talked to God and he's got a special place in heaven for you.' So I'm going to tell you this, Frank Peterson: God has a special place in heaven for you."

"God and the Son," Frank answered.

Santa pulled out a hundred-dollar bill.

"Do you know what this is?" he asked.

"Oh my goodness," Frank said.

"This is for you," Santa said. He explained the Charlie Meyerson name stamped on the bill. "He was a great man and a friend," Santa said.

Santa reached in his pocket for more bills. Slowly, he forked over 10 bills. After the fourth, Frank asked "Oh my goodness, how can you do that?" After the ninth, his mouth hung open.

"It's unbelievable," Frank said before turning toward Maria and enveloping her in a long embrace. "Ma-reeee-a! Oh! Oh!"

In the van afterward, Maria's face glowed.

"This is one of the best adventures I've ever been on," she said.

Santa capped the night by visiting the Gutierrez family. A scam artist claimed he could cure the parents' 18-year-old daughter of a lung disease. He bilked the family out of $2,800, Maria said.

With Maria leading the way, Santa climbed the steps into the family's trailer.

"I understand that a false prophet took some money from you," Santa said, letting Maria translate into Spanish. "We have come to wish you a Merry Christmas and to return that money to you."

Santa gave the mother, Guadalupe Gutierrez, $2,900 to cover the money lost, plus an extra $100. Then he added $500 for Christmas gifts for the children. When the mother said she'd buy her ill daughter a computer for doing school work at home, Santa turned to the girl and handed her $700.

"Computers take printers," Sheriff Tom said.

"Oh, yes," Santa said, adding $300.

Another daughter sitting on a couch covered her face and cried. Tears formed in other family member's eyes. Maria's eyes moistened, too. For about 10 seconds, no one spoke. Some elves fought losing their composure. Someone sniffled.

Santa asked for time alone with the family. Everyone else walked out silently. Santa joined hands with family members in a circle and prayed.

Afterward, Guadalupe called Santa's gift "a miracle."

"He has a beautiful, wonderful heart," she said in Spanish. "I hope that God gives him a long life… We will have a good Christmas. Tell Santa thank you very much. He has been my angel."

Outside, Deputy Maria melted.

Though she hadn't told Santa, Charley also had destroyed the home she rented. She was staying with another deputy who had a spare room. She didn't know when more rental property would be available that she could afford.

In the darkness looking at Santa, none of that mattered. How glad she was now that she had accepted this assignment. She knew who Santa was: an angel.

She couldn't have helped all those people the way he did.

"I have learned the meaning of Christmas this year," she told him as her voice shook and tears fell. "Thank you, thank you."

They embraced.

Thirty-one

'I've never had so much fun'

The next morning, the elves and Santa climbed back into L.D.'s bus for a short drive south. Their minds replayed emotional scenes from the previous night. Hugs from happy recipients. Tears spilled in the Gutierrez home. Fond goodbyes exchanged with Deputy Maria in a Desoto County parking lot.

"I don't know how much more of this I can take," Dick said.

Carefully pulling out of a tight hotel parking lot, L.D. directed the bus toward Port Charlotte, a community of 46,000. There, Santa met a new batch of deputies, including a canine officer and a motorcycle deputy. After pausing for pictures with Dick, they escorted Santa's van into a nearby trailer park that largely resembled a ghost town.

Here, much closer to the coast, the hurricane's wrath became even more apparent. Home after home remained twisted and bent. Half a roof and a third of the walls were missing from one. Others rested on their sides. Street signs tilted at wind-blown angles.

As debris crunched beneath the van's tires, Santa and the elves studied trailer after trailer. Someone had spray-painted names of insurance companies handling claims on many. A large "X" told rescuers in the early hours after the storm that the home already had been searched for victims.

"This whole area was devastated," Deputy Chris Maler said.

Two persons died in the trailer park. Overall, 24 died in Charlotte County, largely a retirement and snowbird community.

As the van turned a corner, Santa spotted 75-year-old Dolores Lowry walking her small dog, Darlin'. The former Pennsylvanian now lived in a FEMA trailer parked next to her peeled home.

Santa jumped out to talk. With a motorcycle officer and patrol car in the caravan, a neighbor worried something bad had happened. She watched as a group surrounded Dolores.

"How is your Christmas going to be?" Santa asked.

"Fine," Dolores answered.

Santa held up a hundred-dollar bill.

"You know what that is?"

"Oh, yes I do. I haven't seen many of them."

Santa gave her two.

"I didn't have insurance," Dolores said later. "What a blessing. It pays to walk my dog."

She gave permission for the group to examine her torn home. For a few minutes, Santa and the elves turned into tourists gawking close-up at Mother Nature's destruction.

Later, after a quick stop at a Salvation Army center, where Christmas toys for needy children were lined up in a large warehouse, Santa asked the deputies if they knew anyone specific who needed assistance.

One deputy mentioned five children in the Lubin family. Their mother had died a year earlier. Their father, injured in a car accident three years earlier, was a paraplegic. Charley had severely damaged their home.

The group drove to the children's school. An elf asked administrators for permission to pull Nordwanna, Sachar, Elijah, Scheyanne and Aunel out of class.

Outside on the asphalt, Santa waited. Within minutes, the children appeared following a secretary. They ranged in age from 16 to 6.

"Your wish list got lost in the mail," Santa told them, "so instead, we brought you these."

He held up cash.

"We figured we'd give you about $1,000."

Captain Ray, who was a big hit because of his firefighter's badge, asked: "Do you believe in Santa Claus now?"

The children nodded.

Santa asked them to raise their right hands. One raised her left hand by mistake. Her siblings laughed. "No, the other hand," one said. Then Santa said: "Repeat after me: I now promise to be an elf of Secret Santa forever." The children repeated it.

They chatted before heading back to class. The sheriff deputies asked the secretary to watch the money for the children.

That afternoon, Santa walked into a small coin-operated laundry in Punta Gorda. Only two people were inside — a man wearing a back brace and a young woman folding clothes.

"Where are you folks from?" Santa asked.

"Cincinnati, Ohio," answered the man, Rick Stallings. The woman looked up but didn't answer. Since Rick hailed from the Midwest, Santa asked if he was a Chicago Bears fan. Dick stood about 20 feet away.

"Why would I be a Bears fan?" Rick asked.

Santa changed the subject.

"We brought a little something for you," he said before handing over a hundred-dollar bill. Stallings looked around. Deputies stood with a small crowd that had gathered behind him.

"Something's wrong," he said. "This kind of stuff don't happen."

Santa turned to the woman and gave her $100, too. "This is for you," he said.

"I just found out I'm two months pregnant," she said. "I can use this."

Rick leaned across a folding table that was between them and offered the woman his hundred-dollar bill. She shook her head and backed away. He dropped the bill on the table and pointed at it.

"Take it," he said. "Pick it up. I got a couple of kids. I know how expensive it is."

Elves gasped.

Santa hesitated then encouraged the woman, Nicole Hogeback of Punta Gorda, to accept the gift. She finally picked it up and shook Rick's hand. "God bless you," she said. Santa turned and gave $200 to Rick.

At another laundry, Santa gave $300 to Jamaican native Eslin Charlton, whose husband was unemployed.

"It has been very difficult," she said. "Thank God. God has provided. God bless you. Praise the Lord."

She waved the money in her hand, high above her head.

"I prayed today," she said. "I pray every day. I'm praying to God to help us along the way…. We didn't have money to buy food this week. Thank God. Thank you Jesus."

Charlie Meyerson's son, Randy, who had joined up with Santa earlier in the day, grinned as he watched.

"I've never had so much fun in my life," he said.

Santa told many recipients, "These aren't Ben Franklins. They are Charlie Meyersons."

Outside, Santa helped two homeless brothers on bicycles, who grinned and shook their heads, amazed. He also spotted a family in a van with a broken window parked near a pharmacy. The couple had three children, including one strapped in a car seat in back. They'd just taken him to a doctor and filled a prescription for his cold. Santa gave them $500.

"Will that help?" Santa asked.

Robert and Tina Williams cried. They said they'd use the money for Christmas gifts.

"When you guys were walking up, I wondered: What did we do?" Tina said, obviously worried by the deputies. "I wasn't expecting this at all. We really appreciate it. For the people who really need it, he is a godsend."

She sobbed, took a breath and started again.

"There's no words to describe how I feel. God bless him and his family."

One of the deputies told Santa about a husband and wife working at an eye clinic in town. They'd lost their house, the deputy said. One worked with medical records, the other performed nighttime maintenance. They had three children, ages 12, 10 and 9.

Santa nodded. Perfect. An elf called ahead to make sure both were working.

Cheryl Barratt came to the lobby first, unsure why visitors asked for her. Santa stepped forward.

"Hi, Cheryl," he said. He wanted to delay until her husband, Richard, arrived, so he asked one of his standard questions.

"Are you a football fan?"

"Yes," she said, "I like the Bears." Her husband was a Patriots fan, though.

"Would you like to meet Dick Butkus some day?" Santa asked. "What if I could get you his autograph?"

Richard walked into the lobby.

"Hi," Santa said, offering a handshake. "I'm Dick Butkus."

Richard laughed.

"You don't believe me?" Santa asked, feigning surprise.

Santa again offered a Dick Butkus autograph and said he knew someone who could make a pretty good copy. He called Dick forward. The Barratts' mouths dropped open. They shook Dick's hand.

"How's Christmas going to be?" Santa asked.

"His parents are going to help us," Cheryl said, pointing to Richard.

Santa pulled out one of his "Charlie Meyerson" bills, explained the name stamped there and asked about the Barratts' children. He gave the family $500.

Charley had ravaged their small home. They huddled in a hallway and listened to their walls breathe, hoping they wouldn't explode. They covered their terrified children with a mattress. The ceiling began to leak.

They had no insurance to cover $41,000 in damage. Their children lost toys and clothes. Yet the day after the storm, their oldest boy helped a neighbor take out the trash.

"We might have lost a lot, but we also grew a lot, too," Richard said.

After visiting another laundry, Santa turned his attention to discount store parking lots. Young workers pushing carts became an easy target. At one point, Santa spotted an elderly couple and headed for them. They weren't married, just friends. She was using a walker.

Santa stepped from the van and offered $100 to Mary Grimm of Port Charlotte. She cried and nearly swooned. Santa reached for her as her friend also put out his hands to catch her. Concerned, Santa stayed and talked for several minutes. When he left, he was five bills lighter. She was $500 richer and more puzzled than ever.

"I can't find an answer to this," she said, clutching her chest. "I lost my husband this year while both of us were in the hospital. They came and told me he died. Now, I'll have to say a lot of prayers asking forgiveness for being mad at the Lord."

In another parking lot, an elf spotted a group of seven persons loading purchases into a rental van. Assuming they'd lost their car in the storm, Santa stopped to help.

Wrong.

They were tourists from England.

"Are we on 'Candid Camera?' " one squealed after getting a hundred-dollar bill. "Who are you? Santa Claus?"

"I can't get over this," another exclaimed. She held up her bill. "I'm going to frame this."

L.D. grinned.

"Isn't America wonderful?" he asked. "Is this your first day here?"

"Yes," one said.

"Well, it won't happen (again) tomorrow," L.D. said.

Everyone laughed.

Thirty-two

Just for Charlie

Even before returning home from Florida, Santa plotted details of his Las Vegas trip, which was just days away. When he told friends, some questioned why he'd pick that city — a glamour and glitz capital packed with high rollers, bright lights and fancy resorts.

But Santa knew about the other side of Vegas — the poorer neighborhoods that housed hotel housekeepers and other low-wage workers. Plenty of needy people lived in Vegas.

Besides, honoring Charlie Meyerson where he worked meant even more to Santa than honoring him in the state where he died. Over the years, Santa had watched Charlie help others in the truest tradition of a Secret Santa. He'd given people money and said, "Now, don't tell anybody." Santa's eyes moistened as he thought about his friend.

He remembered, too, the time in Vegas that Charlie introduced him to Kevyn Wynn, the daughter of casino developer Steve Wynn and his wife, Elaine. Kevyn's parents once paid $1.45 million to get her back from kidnappers, whom authorities later caught, prosecuted and convicted.

As Santa chatted with Kevyn, Charlie had turned to him and asked: "Can I tell her the story?" Charlie liked reciting Santa's story, though he kept mum about Santa's identity. This time, though, he wanted to spill everything.

"Okay," Santa said, nodding.

As Charlie talked, Kevyn's eyes widened.

"Oh, I'd love to go along," she said.

Charlie turned to Santa.

"If you ever come to Las Vegas (as Secret Santa), you have to promise me you will take Kevyn with you."

Santa promised.

Now, it was time to fulfill that promise.

Larry McCormick spearheaded security arrangements. He started by calling hotel security expert Kyle Edwards.

One of Santa's sons agreed to accompany Santa. Dick Butkus said he'd fly in to join them. And after debating the idea for a couple of days, Santa invited a reporter and photographer from the *Las Vegas Review-Journal*. He thought a story might spur others there to be more generous.

§ § §

Less than a week before Christmas, Santa checked into his Las Vegas hotel. He unpacked roughly $35,000, spread it on a marble-top table and invited some of his elves to help him prepare the bills. He grabbed his stamp bearing Charlie's name. He handed the other stamp, bearing the Secret Santa website, to an elf. Others began re-cording serial numbers so that Santa could verify the story if anyone wrote into the website claiming to have received a bill. Dick sat on a nearby couch, a cigar dangling from his mouth, as he re-stacked the stamped bills into $10,000 bundles.

"You remember the movie, 'The Sting?' " Santa asked as he pressed the red-inked stamp onto the back of one bill.

"Yes," an elf said.

"This reminds me a little of that," he said.

§ § §

The next morning at breakfast, Santa studied a typed list of eight families that local law enforcement and others suggested he help. One family was headed by grandparents raising two of their great-grandchildren, a story that resonated with Santa. But then, every family's story tugged at his heart.

Santa explained to his security team that he also would catch people at random along the streets and dart away in the "black getaway car." Two SWAT officers wearing green police fatigues nodded.

"Let's saddle up," Santa told his elves. They headed outdoors into bright sunshine. Most in the group wore long sleeves but no jackets.

Their first stop: the apartment of a Hispanic couple with three children, including a 15-year-old boy with Down syndrome. Santa knocked. Maria Rameriz invited them inside. Her daughter wiggled under the covers of a makeshift bed on the living room floor as her sleepy-eyed brother walked down the hallway to join them.

"We brought something for you all the way from Kansas City," Santa said. He told Maria that he was naming her family "Charlie Meyerson Angels." He pulled out a hundred-dollar bill and showed her the name stamped on it.

"Charlie Meyerson was a dear friend who passed away," Santa said. "We are doing this in his honor."

He counted bills. "One, two, three, four, five, six."

Maria gasped.

"Oh, my gosh," she said.

"I hope that will help," Santa said.

Maria hugged Santa.

"Thank you," she said.

As Santa's group drove toward another apartment, Santa saw a pedestrian hand something to a homeless man pushing a grocery cart of belongings. Santa radioed the escort officers, who flipped on their lights and spun a U-turn across an eight-lane boulevard. Santa's car followed. Santa and the others hopped out.

"We saw what you did," Santa said to the pedestrian, Donald Hayes, a hotel steward originally from Louisiana. "You gave that man some money, didn't you?"

Donald nodded.

"We've got something for you," Santa said, pulling out a bill. "See that name on that bill? What does that say?"

"Charlie Meyerson," Donald said.

"We are doing this in honor of him, in the tradition of the Secret Santa," Santa said. "I've got two more Charlie Meyersons that I'm going to give you."

"Good Lord, have mercy," Donald said. "Lord, Jesus."

Donald thanked Santa and explained that he needed to take his boy Christmas shopping. His last paycheck had been only $400, he said.

"I'd like to frame this," he said, holding up one of the bills, "but God knows I need it."

Donald looked at the officers and police car.

"You turned your lights on, and I thought I was going to get harassed," he said. He laughed now at the thought.

Across the street, a man's van stalled as he pulled onto the boulevard. The elves and Santa trotted across the boulevard to push it back into a lot. Another man saw what they were doing and helped. Santa rewarded him with $100. The van's owner, Antoine Francese, a French-speaking man from North Africa, had just bought the used van. Santa gave him $1,100.

When they reached the apartment of an 11-year-old crime witness, an officer explained in Spanish to the girl's mother why they had come. The mother, Tarlota Soto, invited them inside. A small Christmas tree, sparsely decorated, stood in one corner. Her daughter, Dhiodara, was away, she said. They came to Las Vegas after Tarlota's husband, a police officer, was killed in Mexico. One day, her daughter was buying treats from an ice cream truck driver when two robbers pushed her aside, shot the driver and robbed him. Her daughter identified the robbers for Las Vegas authorities.

"We brought something for you from Kansas City," Santa began, using one of his favorite opening sentences. "We are, uh, the Secret Santa. These are my elves. We know what you went through. We really support law enforcement."

An officer translated Santa's words into Spanish.

"Gracias," Tarlota answered.

"Your family has been selected to receive the Charlie Meyerson Spirit Award," Santa said. "With that comes an honorarium."

He counted each bill as he handed them to her — 15 in all. She began to cry.

"Muchas gracias," she said before wiping first one eye then the other. She spilled more words in Spanish.

"She's very thankful," the translator told Santa.

Santa nodded. "You tell your daughter that she is my hero," he said.

Later, outside Elaine Wynn Elementary School, Santa met up with Kevyn Wynn. For several minutes, they stood by the trunk of his car, exchanging stories about Charlie. Santa's eyes watered. Kevyn put her hand on his shoulder and consoled him.

Santa reached into his trunk and pulled out a bottle marked "Charlie Meyerson's special formula." When the manufacturer discontinued Charlie's favorite cologne, Charlie coerced an executive into making him a special batch. He had given some to Santa, who fanned the money he'd brought and asked Kevyn to spray cologne on it. When she finished, he turned to his elves and announced: "Saddle up."

After they hit a bus stop, Kevyn spotted a Jack in the Box and suggested they go inside.

"How many have you got working here today?" Santa asked a clerk. A supervisor saw the news photographer and a video cameraman, whom Santa had brought from Kansas City, standing behind Santa. She shook her head.

"We can't answer any questions," she said.

Santa held out a hundred-dollar bill. "We have one for each of your employees," he pleaded.

"That's okay," she answered, waving him off.

"It's for Christmas, ma'am."

"I'm sorry."

Santa sighed. "See how hard it is sometimes," he told the newer elves. "And we have police officers with us."

Santa changed tactics and ordered a diet Coke. He plopped a bill on the counter and told the clerk to keep the change. The clerk shook his head.

"It's a charity donation," one of the officers said.

"We are here to give each of your employees $100 for Christmas," Santa added.

The clerk laughed.

"That's for you," Santa said.

"Really, I cannot accept it," the clerk said.

The manager picked up a phone to call her superiors. No cameras were allowed in the restaurant without permission, another worker explained. Santa asked the photographers to go outside. Finally, after all that, the employees accepted his money.

A few miles away, Santa entered a Goodwill second-hand store packed with holiday shoppers. Three or four clerks rang up purchases near the doors. Santa walked past them into busy aisles and began stuffing folded bills into people's hands.

"I couldn't believe it," a woman with a cane exclaimed.

Toward the back of the store, Santa handed $100 to a petite woman browsing clothing racks. In Spanish, she explained that she had four children, the oldest in college studying psychology. She said she would use Santa's money toward rent.

"Here, we have some more," Santa said, handing her 10 more bills.

"Gracias, senõr," she said. She began to cry. She hugged Santa and his son, who had been translating. Behind them, Kevyn called her mother to tell her what was happening.

"What are you doing?" her mother asked.

"Crying," Kevyn answered.

Santa gave away nearly $3,000 inside the Goodwill store.

After stopping at two more apartments, Santa arrived at the home of Arthur Schwartz, who quit work to care for his wife, who had multiple sclerosis. A broken motorized wheelchair sat near his front door. It needed $8,000 worth of repairs, Arthur told Santa as they entered. Santa gave him $4,000.

By then, it was nearly 2 p.m. and time to pick up another elf. The caravan headed to Butch Harmon's golf school. Inside, pictures of Butch's most famous former student, Tiger Woods, adorned a wall.

"How's your health?" Butch asked Santa.

"Never been better," Santa answered.

Butch gave the elves a quick tour before joining them to watch Santa work. Down the road, they spotted a landscaping crew. Santa's son jumped out, wished each person a Merry Christmas and handed out $800.

Near a bus stop, Santa saw a man wearing a Santa hat, a natural target. The caravan stopped. Santa handed the man $100 and asked, "Where are you from?"

"Chicago."

Santa grinned and began talking Bears football. Of course, Elf No. 51 stood nearby in street clothes. Another man at the bus stop suddenly spotted Dick and declared, "I don't believe it. It's him!"

The men swarmed Dick, who signed autographs while Santa continued giving money to others nearby. Dick handed one young teen an autograph, pointed to Santa and whispered something.

The boy walked toward Santa.

"What will you give me for this?" he asked, holding up the autograph.

Santa chuckled.

"I'll give you $100."

The boy's eyes grew as big as saucers. Santa handed him the money, looked at the autograph again and said, "Aw, I've already got one of those. You keep it."

As the sun's rays began to fade, Santa stopped at the home of a quadriplegic. She had gone to the hospital to visit someone, but her roommate, Lucy, was home. Santa gave Lucy $400 and asked her to give it to the other woman when she returned. Santa started to leave but Dick stopped him and said, "Hey, this is the lady who takes care of her."

"Oh, yeah," Santa said. "How could I have missed that one?"
He handed Lucy $400 for herself. Lucy's mouth fell open.

"Who is this from?" she asked.

"Secret Santa in Kansas City."

"Well, thank you. This is so unexpected."

After dark, Santa finally arrived at the apartment of the grandparents who were raising two great-grandchildren. They warmly invited his group inside and offered everyone seats. Santa preferred to stand.

"We come to bring you Christmas presents," he said.

"How come?" the grandmother asked.

"You have some friends at the police department," Santa said.

Santa asked about the grandsons, who were 11 and 8 but not home at the moment. After mentioning that he was raised by his grandparents, Santa gave the couple $1,000.

One of the local elves told Santa about homeless shelters. The caravan headed toward them. A long line of men waited to enter the men's shelter. An equally long line of women and children waited to stay at the 414-bed Shade Tree family shelter. Many carried bags of clothes or pushed grocery carts packed with belongings — a wrenching sight.

Santa entered the Shade Tree and announced he had brought a cash donation from Kansas City. The person who took donations had left for the day, an employee said.

"Can you get in touch with her?" Santa asked.

Miles away at an outlet mall, Brenda Dizon's cell phone rang as she shopped for her husband's Christmas presents. "Secret Santa wants to see you," a Shade Tree employee said. Brenda didn't understand.

"Who?" she asked.

"You need to come back," the employee said.

When Brenda arrived 10 minutes later, she saw the SWAT officers and briefly worried why they were there — until she realized they were with Santa. She told Santa a little about the shelter, including that its motto was, "Hope, safety and opportunity," and that it provided beds for 80,000 women and children a year on a budget of

$1.7 million.

"If you figure that out, that's about $21 a day per person," Brenda said. "You can't get much more cost effective than that."

She offered Santa a brochure.

He offered her $5,000.

"I'm sure you are going to put this to great use," he said. "I appreciate all the work you do. God bless you and Merry Christmas."

After years in the business, very few things surprised Brenda. This was one of them. She stood with her mouth ajar, wondering if she really heard what Santa just said. He counted out the bills. She hugged him.

"Every single donation helps, but some are more special than others," she said later. "When you have someone come to your city from out of town and say, 'We want to help,' that's pretty darn special."

His day done, Santa said goodbye to the security detail and headed back toward the ritzy Las Vegas strip. Bright lights flashed past their car windows. A passenger in Santa's car mentioned something about money and how "you can't take it with you."

"It's absolutely no fun" having it, Santa answered, "if you can't share it."

SANTA'S SECRET: A STORY OF HOPE

Thirty-three

Footprints in the snow

S anta arrived at Kansas City Fire Station No. 2 to give money to two families chosen by the firefighters. One recipient shook his hand and asked: "What's your name?"

"My name," Santa began, "is not important."

Santa explained the Tvedten Angel award and why each family had been selected. "We always do this in cash," he said. "It comes from the heart of the firefighters."

He handed $1,000 to one family and $1,100 to the other.

"Merry Christmas and God bless you," he said.

Turning to the reporters, photographers and elves waiting nearby, Santa added, "Now we've got some sleigh riding to do."

Smiles broke out among the firefighters. Santa's sleigh would have to wait.

They took Santa to a room alongside the truck bay. About the size of a small bedroom, it contained old furniture, including a mattress on box springs. Firefighter Charlie Cashen knew Santa liked music, played the guitar and sometimes penned his own lyrics. Charlie played the guitar and, through a stroke of luck, had repurchased a Gibson guitar he once owned.

Charlie showed it to Santa. "This is for you," Charlie said.

Santa's eyes lit up. He gently took the guitar in his large hands and sat down on the mattress. His right thumb strummed the strings. He checked the tune. His fingers moved again. A mix of chords spilled from the guitar.

Santa began to sing in a Southern, country-western voice.

He walked in this Dixie Diner, more than 30 years ago.
No money in his pocket, and no place he could go.
His name he kept a secret, he was so ashamed,
of being broke and homeless, and feeling hunger pain.

A Mississippi diner, his shelter from the cold.
In this place, a frightened face, that wasn't very old.
The man behind the counter said "Have a front-row seat.
Folks 'round here just call me Ted; what'll you have to eat."

"I'll just try some grits and gravy, if that's all right with you."
But Ted fixed him up a breakfast that was big enough for two.
As the young man nursed his coffee, he closed his eyes to pray.
God help me I need lifting up, I'm way too low today.

Then right out of nowhere, a Christmas dream came true.
Ted said "I found this twenty, and it must belong to you."
His heart said not to take it, but fear gave him no choice.
And on the road he prayed this vow, with his trembling voice.

He said, "Someday I will repay, the kindness I've been shown.
I will help the hungry, and those who are alone.
I'll be a Secret Santa, and my gifts will always be,
the kind that lets them all hang onto their dignity."

A lady in a laundry late night Christmas Eve,
A cold and hungry soldier living on the street,
young family in a pawn shop, broken down old truck.
A mother knelt in prayer for God to change their luck.

Then a stranger out of nowhere, a man who gets his thrills,
by filling people's pockets with hundred-dollar bills.
At Christmas time you will find him somewhere on a street.
Passing on the kindness that once fell at his feet.

Last week the Dixie Diner was just about to close.
In walked a gray-haired stranger, dressed in Christmas clothes.
An older yet still trembling voice, we all heard him say,
"I'm looking for a man named Ted, there's a debt I must repay."

He handed Ted that twenty, and then ten thousand more.
And all he said was "Pray for me, I could always use some more."

Folks call him Secret Santa, they never know his name.
He helps the broke and homeless, and those with hunger pain.
So if your heart needs lifting up, just close your eyes and pray,
and his footprints in the snow just might lead your way.

He struck the last chord and let the sound drift away. For a few seconds, no one spoke.

Grinning, Santa looked at Charlie.

"Thank you," he said.

"You're welcome," Charlie said, smiling too.

Then Santa dashed into bright daylight outside, trailed by his elves.

It was time to make a different kind of music.

SANTA'S SECRET: A STORY OF HOPE

Thirty-four
Ted's turn for fun

Ted Horn, by now a widower approaching his 88th birthday, received word in the fall of 2005 that Secret Santa would be making another dash through Mississippi in December. This time, Santa wanted to help victims of Hurricane Katrina.

A Mississippi native, Santa felt sick over what had happened to the Magnolia State. New Orleans grabbed more media attention after Katrina destroyed much of that below-sea-level city in Louisiana, but the storm devastated Mississippi, too.

It cut a massive swath inland in late August, snapping trees, soaking houses and smashing buildings into Paul Bunyan-size kindling. Even residents living along Mississippi's northern border suffered through days without electricity. Along the coast, the storm surge rose a foot an hour, cresting as high as 28 feet. It swept one police department's entire fleet into the Gulf of Mexico.

In the first days afterward, Santa could do little except send money through relief agencies. He decided to visit the state later, closer to Christmas.

In November, he called Ted in Tupelo and asked permission to stop by the first weekend in December. He wondered: Could Ted fix him breakfast again?

The idea tickled Ted so much that he talked about the impending visit every day for weeks. He said he'd fry some eggs and sausage, just like in 1971, when a hungry, homeless and penniless Santa ordered a big breakfast at the Dixie Diner.

Santa and his entourage arrived a little before noon on a cloudy

Saturday. A Mississippi Highway Patrol car turned slowly onto the block first, followed by a caravan of four vehicles and another Highway Patrol car. They passed neatly manicured yards surrounding modest ranch-style homes.

Standing in his carport, Ted leaned on a black cane and watched the motorcade arrive. His son and daughter and other family members stood alongside. They grinned as the cars pulled up and people popped out.

Wearing his usual red flannel shirt, Santa strode up the driveway, chuckling about a prank Cecil had just helped him play on an elf during their drive from the Memphis airport. He reached to shake Ted's hand.

"Hi, buddy," Santa said. "Good to see ya."

Neighbors stared at the crowd. One woman feared that something had happened to Ted, but a Highway Patrol trooper assured her that Mr. Horn was all right.

Another neighbor looked out his front window and fixed his gaze on a tall gentleman with a flattop haircut and a limp. He looked familiar, like that retired NFL player who'd coached a Pennsylvania high school football team as ESPN viewers watched in the fall.

"That's Dick Butkus," the neighbor told his grandson. "Go get my binoculars."

The Horns exchanged pleasantries with Santa and his elves before Santa turned to Ted and announced: "We heard this was a restaurant."

Ted nodded. He had a tea kettle on the stove and breakfast ready to cook.

"I'll pay you after I eat," Santa quipped. "I think I paid you with your own money last time."

When Santa first visited Ted's home six years earlier, he entered through the front door, like a stranger. This time, he and the elves walked through the carport and in a side door, like family.

Plates and bowls of chicken wings, roasted pecans and other snacks filled one end of the kitchen counter. A griddle set on the stove's back burner, ready to be heated. Coffee cups idled on saucers, ready to be filled.

Ted poured coffee for Dick, who parked himself on a stool at the kitchen counter and prodded Ted to talk about 1971. Why, Dick asked, had a much younger Ted helped a much younger Santa all those years ago?

"He was just a pitiful little thing," Ted answered. "He was skin and bones then."

Two fresh eggs sizzled alongside two sausage patties on the grill.

"He gave me $10,000," Ted said. "You know that?"

"What did you do with the money?"

"Good Lord. I didn't know what to do with it."

"Did you think it was a joke?"

"No."

Santa took the stool next to Dick.

"Hey, Cookie," he said to Ted. "Where's my coffee?"

Ted poured him coffee, flipped the eggs onto their yolks and stirred the grits. He remarked that he wasn't as nimble at juggling all that food as in the old days.

"Mr. Butkus might want some of those grits," Santa said, teasing his tall friend. Dick didn't grow up on Southern food like Santa. No, he didn't want any grits.

Ted served Santa the eggs, sausage, toast and grits, along with more coffee. Santa asked for the sugar bowl. Ted's daughter, Sandra Cox, gasped.

"Don't tell me you put sugar in your grits," she said. "That's not a true Southerner."

"Now wait a minute," Santa said. "My grandpa taught me this."

"Really?" Sandra asked.

"Some people put sugar and cocoa in them," Ted said. "Have you tried that?"

"I have," Santa said. "I definitely have."

Ted slipped a hundred-dollar bill next to Santa's plate, so that Santa could once again pay for his breakfast with Ted's money.

"You must have dropped this," Ted said, replaying an old line.
Chatter filled the room as the elves, troopers and Ted's family talked and ate. Someone asked Cecil to explain what happened earlier, in the van with Dick. Cecil grinned. He'd been wearing the wig and fake hillbilly teeth plus some really old, dirty and holey clothes. Santa had asked him to wait in a Tupelo parking lot with a handmade sign that said, "Need help." When Santa drove past, Santa whipped into the lot and began asking Cecil questions, as if they were strangers. Dick asked Cecil questions, too. Cecil made up stories about digging potatoes and needing a ride across town. When Santa offered him a ride, Cecil climbed into the van and sat behind Dick. Using a hillbilly accent, he asked Dick all kinds of questions as they drove a few more blocks to Ted's place. When they parked, Cecil reached forward and offered his hand to Dick to shake. Dick had planned to barely touch Cecil's dirty hand when he looked back and noticed that the homeless tramp had cleaned up. Cecil's wig and fake teeth were gone. Cecil grinned at Dick, who stared, dumbfounded.

"Oh, man!" Dick said.

Santa burst out in laughter.

Now, Sandra asked Santa whether his breakfast was as good as the one her dad fixed him in 1971.

"Well, it's great," Santa said. "But the other one was much more memorable."

A few minutes later, Santa tapped a knife against a glass. The room quieted.

Santa mentioned a song recently recorded in Nashville by some friends Santa met when they were aspiring song writers and musicians and he was a teenage janitor, cleaning the studio after them. He'd recently asked them a favor, to record this new song.

"I call it the Ted Horn song," Santa explained. "I titled it 'Footprints in the Snow.' So, Mr. Horn, this is the first copy that anybody's got. You're going to keep that…. I want you to enjoy it, I hope you do."

Sandra plugged in a portable compact disc player, slid in the disc and hit the play button. A man's voice wafted through the room. *He walked in this Dixie Diner, more than 30 years ago. No money in his pocket, and no place he could go. His name he kept a secret, he was so ashamed. Of being broke and homeless and feeling hunger pain...*

It was the same song, with a few tweaks, that Santa had sung while playing Charlie Cashen's old guitar in a Kansas City fire station a year earlier. Now, it was Ted's turn to hear the song, but without the guitar accompaniment.

...The man behind the counter said have a front-row seat. Folks 'round here just call me Ted, what'll you have to eat...

Standing behind Santa, Ted smiled.

The crowd in his house — friends and strangers alike — listened without saying a word. This was Santa's story, one nearly everyone in the room knew well, but few had heard the song.

...Then right out of nowhere, a Christmas dream came true. Ted said 'I found this twenty, and it must belong to you.'

Ted's action helped Santa become Secret Santa. And though the song's words took literary license with the events, they told a story that wove Ted and Santa together forever.

...Last week the Dixie Diner was just about to close. In walked a gray-haired stranger, dressed in Christmas clothes. An older yet still trembling voice, we all heard him say, 'I'm looking for a man named Ted, there's a debt I must repay.' He handed Ted that twenty, and then ten thousand more. And all he said was, 'Pray for me, I could always use some more.'

Folks call him Secret Santa, they never know his name. He helps the broke and homeless, and those with hunger pain. So if your heart needs lifting up, just close your eyes and pray. And his footprints in the snow, just might lead your way.

The music stopped. Gentle applause filled the room. People looked at Ted.

"It's an amazing story," he said softly. "People everywhere know about it now. A lot of times, I'll be signing my check, and people will say, 'Hold on, that name sounds familiar.' And then they'll remember the Secret Santa."

Santa grinned.

"You're about to get a little more famous," he said.

"How's that?"

Santa looked around for Sheriff Tom.

"Sheriff?"

"Right behind you."

Sheriff Tom stepped forward and handed something to Santa, who suggested they move to the dining room. Once there, Santa dumped $50,000 on the table and asked Ted to help him with a little chore. Santa had a special stamp, and he wanted Ted to use it to stamp the back of some of the hundred-dollar bills.

Ted looked surprised when the red letters appeared on the first Ben Franklin.

"What does that say?" Santa asked.

"Ted Horn," Ted answered.

The previous year, Santa had honored another friend by stamping the bills with that friend's name. This year, he wanted to honor Ted throughout Mississippi.

"My kinfolks down on the coast might see one of these," Ted said as he stamped.

When they finished, Santa counted 10 bills and handed them to Ted.

"I want you to find somebody that needs it," he said. "You give it to whoever you choose."

First, though, Santa wanted to visit the Dixie Diner one more time with Ted. The old sign still hung above the brick building, where the current operator still served $5 haircuts.

When Santa's van pulled up outside the old diner, a dark-haired man got out of a nearby white car. John Raucci, special agent in charge of the FBI for Mississippi, had been waiting. He shook Santa's hand, eager to watch him work.

Ted posed for pictures in front of the old diner as word spread quickly through town that two highway patrol cars were parked there. Santa entered the shop and "paid" the barber enough for 20 haircuts, but he didn't tarry long enough to test the barber's chair.

"This was the whole diner," Santa explained to John.

"The grill was right where the mirror is," Ted added. "The kitchen was back there." He pointed behind a wall.

As they said good-bye outside the old diner, Ted told Santa: "Let's do this every year." They hugged.

In the days that followed, Ted contemplated how to distribute Santa's money.

One morning, he awoke and said a prayer, asking for guidance. He opened his Bible to the reading his church had recommended for that day: 2 Corinthians 9:6-15, from a letter written by the Apostle Paul.

The point is this: the one who sows sparingly will also reap sparingly, and the one who sows bountifully will also reap bountifully. Each of you must give as you have made up your mind, not reluctantly or under compulsion, for God loves a cheerful giver.

That morning, Ted indeed felt like a cheerful giver.

He headed to his bank. Reluctant to hand out bills bearing his own name, he withdrew $1,000 from his account in fifty-dollar bills. The smaller bills would go further, he reasoned.

Outside the bank, he saw a man with his trunk open and hood up. Ted approached and asked the man what was wrong. The man grumbled about his carburetor not working properly.

"Looks like I'll have to buy a new one," the man said.

Ted pulled $50 from his pocket.

"Will this help?" he asked.

The man hesitated before accepting. Joy spilled across his face. Warmth washed over Ted.

"God bless you, God bless you," the man said over and over.

Later, when Sandra learned what her father had done, she warned him to be careful. "Don't have a whole wad of the fifties in your hand," she said. "Just have one in your pocket where you can pull one out. And don't pull up where there's a crowd."

199

Two mornings later, Sandra called her father but got no answer. She waited a bit and tried again. Still no answer. She considered calling one of his neighbors to check on him but decided first to try his cell phone.

He answered.

"Where are you?" Sandra asked.

He was outside the mall, wearing a red elf hat Santa had given him, driving around, looking for people who needed money.

"If they can go to the mall, they probably don't need money," Sandra said, reminding her dad that Secret Santa liked laundries, thrift stores and "places like that."

Ted drove to Sonic with his mind set on a $50 breakfast sandwich. Before he pulled in, he prayed that whichever young girl came to the car would be someone who needed money.

A teenager with stringy, unkempt hair delivered his food.

"Do you believe in Santa Claus?" Ted asked.

"Yes sir. I do."

He paid with a $50 and told her to keep the change. She went inside but soon returned.

"Sir, did you mean for me to keep all of this?"

"Yes."

She cried.

"Thank you, thank you," she said.

Over the next days, with Sandra's help, Ted gave away his $1,000 — and had so much fun that he distributed Santa's $1,000, too. He helped a family that lost everything in a house fire. He gave to eight low-income single mothers he knew through their child-care provider. He handed money to a man with a bad back who'd been laid off work three weeks earlier. He found four car hops at Bumpers Drive-In and some Hispanic workers with low-wage jobs.

One recipient wrote him a note and called him a "sweet, special man" and said that the Secret Santa story had changed her outlook on life and made her want to be a better person.

Giving away money made Ted feel good. The look on people's

faces — Ted couldn't explain it, but it was special.

"I'm like Santa," he said afterward. "I got hooked."

SANTA'S SECRET: A STORY OF HOPE

Thirty-five

After Hurricane Katrina

After leaving Ted in Houston, Santa headed deeper south, still escorted by troopers. Three months after Hurricane Katrina plowed through their state, the gloomy aftermath remained fresh in the troopers' minds.

Steve Gladney, a lieutenant in the Mississippi Highway Patrol, was stationed about 240 miles inland when the storm struck. Driving to the coast afterward, he encountered so much debris it took 10 hours to cover 170 miles. The Mississippi Department of Transportation summoned bulldozers and chainsaw operators to clear routes.

Near the coast, troopers encountered a mess of stinky mud, uprooted trees and destroyed structures. In some places, if the winds didn't tear off roofs, powerfully driven rain soaked through walls. Officers from one police department huddled in a hurricane-proof library, thinking they would be safe, but then the storm surge began to fill the building, and they feared they would drown. One tried shooting out a window, but the hurricane-proof glass refused to break. Eventually, the storm's pressure blew open an escape route. Some of the officers survived by climbing and clinging to trees, Steve said.

Steve said the storm surge destroyed some neighborhoods so thoroughly, only overturned cars remained recognizable afterward. John with the FBI likened the scene to the damage from of an atomic bomb, minus the heat.

Winds also blew over Highway Patrol cell towers, leaving troopers no way to reach dispatchers or tell their families they were safe. Much of the state also lost electricity, meaning no air-conditioning, no refrigeration and no traffic lights, among other things. More than

230 people died.

"We were handing out water to families who lost everything," Steve recalled, "and you'd think we were handing out hundred-dollar bills, they were so grateful."

This early December day, after stopping in Tupelo and Houston, the troopers and John escorted Santa south along the Natchez Trace Parkway to the town of Kosciusko, the birthplace of Oprah Winfrey. After a late dinner, Santa and his elves called it a night.

The next morning, they started at Freddie's Restaurant, where two waitresses were surprised to have a crowd outside when they unlocked the doors at 7 a.m. Steam rose from scrambled eggs, sausage and grits on the breakfast bar.

After he ate, Santa stood and asked: "Which elf has been with me the longest?"

Someone pointed to Sheriff Tom.

Santa looked through a stack of red felt hats, patterned off the Ben Hogan golf hat, and handed one to Tom. Then Santa distributed similar hats to Dick Butkus, Ray Wynn and others.

The waitresses wondered about the fuss and asked what was going on. Someone pointed to Dick and said, "He's famous." One waitress walked over, leaned down and asked Dick if that was true. Dick shook his head and pointed across the table to Santa. "He's the famous one," Dick joked.

A little later, Santa went to the cash register to pay his bill. When a reporter followed to pay, she noticed both waitresses wiping tears from their eyes.

"What happened?" the reporter asked, having a pretty good idea what the answer would be.

Santa had given each of them $100, the women said. When they cried, he gave each of them another $100. They hardly could believe it. Both were grandparents, and one had been fighting medical problems since March.

"It was a blessing," Debra Mann said.

Outside, Santa's elves paused for a photograph. One of the waitresses, finally aware of who Dick was, dashed outside and asked him for an autograph. She beamed as he signed.

Later, a few miles outside of town, Santa's motorcade pulled off a roadway onto a long gravel drive behind a car driven by Santa's former high school football coach, David Oakes. Coach climbed the porch steps and knocked. No one answered.

A single mother with seven children lived in the house, Coach said. She had been widowed three times. As others talked about leaving, Coach walked around to the back door and knocked again. He shouted: "They're here."

Everyone inside had been asleep. It was, after all, only 8:15 on a Sunday morning, and the family had been up late the previous night.

Santa and the elves waited near the front porch while mom and the children dressed. As the children came outside a few at a time, the elves began asking their names and ages. Twelve-year-old Jordan, the third oldest, wore a cast on his left arm, the result of a four-wheeler accident two weeks earlier.

"Was it your four-wheeler?" an elf asked.

"No," Jordan said. "It belonged to someone else."

When all five boys and two girls had joined their mother on the porch, Santa told them: "We came all this way from Kansas City to see you. We're sent by Secret Santa. He's this guy who goes around and finds folks to do something special for. We work for him."

He pointed to Coach and added, "Here's one of our elves."

The phone rang inside.

"My phone's ringing off the hook," Genny Bohrer said. "Any time there's this many cars in my driveway, my neighbors assume someone has died."

Santa asked the children what they wanted for Christmas before handing $100 to each and giving $500 to Genny. Santa pointed out the name on the bills and got the children to say "Ted Horn" in unison.

Someone asked the kids if they believed in Santa Claus.

"Santa Claus isn't real," answered one of the boys. "We know the real meaning of Christmas. It's Jesus."

One of the girls added: "We believe in Ted Horn."

Everyone laughed.

As Santa turned to go, Genny said: "Thank you from the bottom of my heart. It's real special to know that there are people who really care."

Santa returned to nearby Kosciusko and gave $1,000 to Pat Rice at the Helping Hands Ministries, an emergency food and clothing agency run by volunteers in an old gymnasium. It had provided food, kitchen utensils, pillows, blankets and other household items to hundreds of hurricane evacuees. More donations filled the warehouse, including toys.

"I'm speechless," Pat said. "I've never heard of anything like this."

The caravan loaded up and headed south. One of Santa's support vehicles was driven by Kansas City Fire Department Captain Mick Byrne, who had volunteered in Mississippi for six weeks after Katrina struck. As the terrain passed, he noticed many damaged trees remained tilted at odd angles, their roots tugged from the ground. But the worst of the debris had been removed, and the landscape looked much cleaner now.

When he first arrived after the storm, Mick was given a FEMA shirt to wear, but people were so hostile toward FEMA that Mick and his co-workers changed into fire department t-shirts after two days. They distributed food and helped sign up people for temporary housing in trailers.

"They didn't feel FEMA was doing anything," Mick recalled. "They calmed down when we told them we were firefighters just trying to help. Everybody got nice then."

He met many families who didn't live on much before the storm and had even less after it. Many spent what little money they had on gasoline to keep generators running. Others had moved in with friends, sometimes jamming 15 or 20 people into one small house.

As Mick knocked on doors deep in rural areas weeks after the storm, he found some people who still hadn't received help. Often, their phone and electricity remained out. One woman had walked four miles to a neighbor's house to get a horse to ride into town so she could get food. One man was living in a shed that reeked of gasoline. When Mick asked why, the man explained he poured gasoline around the outside to keep the snakes away.

When Mick spotted an older woman on her porch, he said, "Hi. What are you doing?" She answered: "Well, I was just praying that someone would bring me some food."

As Mick recalled the stories, he wondered how those people were doing now.

§ § §

After a long drive, Santa's caravan arrived at Wiggins, a small county seat town about 35 miles from the coast. One week earlier, two of the town's police officers were shot and killed while responding to a 911 call. When Santa heard about it from John, he knew he had to stop in Wiggins, even if the town hadn't been on his original route.

They met Wiggins Police Chief Buddy Bell inside a city building. The chief wore a black mourning band across the front of his badge. He shook Santa's hand then looked at Dick and said, "You look bigger on television." Dick laughed.

Santa asked the chief what had happened a week earlier.

"Last Sunday night, two of my officers responded to a domestic open-line call. A few minutes passed with no communication, so additional officers were sent. My two officers were victims."

Officer Brandon Breland, 23, had been with the department two years. Officer Odel Fite, 48, had worked in Augusta before coming to Wiggins. Both were shot twice.

"They will be greatly missed by our department," the chief said in a slow Southern drawl that emphasized his sadness. "That one blow took 20 percent of our police department away from us that night."

"We are sorry to hear about that," Santa said. He explained that in Kansas City, a special fund helps families of police and other emergency workers who die in the line of duty.

"If we left a little gift for you, will you see it gets to the right place?" Santa asked.

The chief nodded.

Santa explained Ted Horn's name on the bills then counted out $5,000, handing each bill one at a time to the chief, who shook his head in disbelief. A fund the department had started for the two families had raised about $1,000 for each family.

"We're really sorry for your loss," Santa said.

"My department and I thank you very much," the chief said. "Thank you from the bottom of my heart."

He started to choke up. Santa asked how long he had been chief.

"Since July 5th of this year. I went through one major storm, the death of my father and the death of two officers.... If I had known all the heartaches, I don't know if I would have said yes or not."

§ § §

Santa's caravan turned west for 24 miles and pulled into Poplarville, one of the towns Mick knew from his volunteer work. Outside a store, Santa spotted a woman with two kids in a rusted car. He handed her $200.

"Oh, my God!" she exclaimed. "I get my roof."

In another parking lot, Santa gave $200 to Martha Hume, who was loading her husband's wheelchair into a van.

"We lost everything in our house due to the water," she said. "This means I get to replace a few more things."

Mick spotted a 52-year-old man in a motorized wheelchair leaving the parking lot, so he chased him in the van. Mick asked the man to wait while Santa caught up. Santa gave the man $100 and wished him Merry Christmas.

Later, Santa asked a woman how she was faring. She complained about fighting her insurance company to fix their roof. Santa gave her money, too.

At a nearby service station, Santa bought a snack and told the clerk: "We're kind of in a hurry, so why don't you keep the change."

"Is he for real?" asked Brittany Kelly. "He just gave me $89.33. Is there a catch?"

Assured there wasn't, Brittany said, "Thank you — and thank God."

Each worker at a nearby Sonic received $100, about 17 hours worth of pay, according to one 17-year-old who started to cry.

Wanting to see the shore before sunset, Santa's caravan headed south to Gulfport, about 45 miles away. The troopers took them to a spot along the beach where a row of mansions once faced the gulf. Only crumbled foundations and tumbled trees remained. Trash littered the shore. Much more lay hidden beneath the waves.

As the sun vanished below the horizon, the caravan turned and headed to a local Wal-Mart. Cars packed the lot, but Santa couldn't tell the needy from the well-to-do. Too many of the cars looked fairly new.

In the next lot, Dick spotted a man wearing an Illinois hat sitting outside a beat-up 1978 Dodge conversion van. Santa drove up, parked and struck up a conversation with Russell Buchanan, who said he was 72. He lived in the van, which had a tattered bicycle affixed to the back.

Russell lacked most of his front teeth and professed to being retired. Santa tried to hand him $500, saying "Here, you dropped this." Russell didn't buy it.

"I didn't drop that!" he said.

"We're from Kansas City," Santa said. "We work for this guy who goes around at Christmas and helps people out sometimes and spreads a little Christmas cheer."

"You sure did it tonight," Russell said, taking the money. "The Lord is going to bless you. We'll be able to use this at the food bank."

Santa looked surprised and asked if Russell was going to give the money away.

"I don't spend my money for anything," he said. "When you drove

209

up, I was trying to decide whether to get a cheap hamburger. But nah, I've got a couple of Vienna sausages."

By now, it was well after dark, and Santa had hotel reservations well inland, at Jackson. The caravan loaded up and said goodbye to the coast.

Near Mount Olive, the group stopped for gasoline. As usual, Santa surprised the workers inside. Back outside, near the pumps, he saw Angie Sullivan gassing an old Ford Ranger.

"We came by to say Merry Christmas," Santa said.

"Why?" asked Angie, who cleaned houses.

"Because we're here from Kansas City and we work for Secret Santa."

Santa handed her $300.

"Ya'all going to make me cry," Angie said. "Wow."

§ § §

The next morning, troopers escorted Santa through Jackson. Santa spotted someone who looked homeless in a parking lot and handed him $100. The man promised to give half to the Salvation Army. Of course, that prompted Santa to reach in his pocket again and hand over four more bills.

"It's amazing," Joe Shanks said afterward. "God is good all the time."

Santa gave $800 to a homeless shelter. Three seamstresses working in the back room got $100 each.

"Sometimes we don't make that much in a whole month," one said.

Tipped by a friend, Santa stopped at the Stuart C. Irby Company, which handles electrical supplies. About a dozen workers were in the warehouse. They gathered as Dick handed each $100. Santa explained the Ted Horn story and began leading a cheer.

"Who's on that bill?"

"Ted Horn!" the workers yelled.

Who?"

"Ted Horn!"

Rodney Kendrick, who had lost a leg in a 1981 car accident, called his gift a blessing. "God got my attention (in 1981) and he got it again right now," Rodney said.

Another worker had asked his wife the previous night what she wanted for Christmas. When she mentioned boots, he said he'd have to wait until payday arrived Friday. Now, he didn't have to wait.

Santa glanced at his watch. Soon, the caravan needed to head back toward Memphis, but he wanted to help at least one more charity. John called Mayor Frank Melton, who suggested the YMCA, which ran a day care for poor families.

The mayor met Santa at the facility. Santa counted out $5,000.

"We brought $50,000 to distribute in Mississippi, and we don't want to take it home," Santa explained.

Before leaving the city, Santa walked into the Greyhound station, which was next to the train station. He distributed bills to a few folks sitting around then noticed a man sleeping on a bench. Santa put $100 on the man, who sat up and asked, "Is this for real?"

Julius Nuss said he had come to Mississippi to find his children, who stayed with their mother after the two of them divorced. Unable to find the children, Julius planned to return to Cheyenne, Wyoming, where he sometimes stayed at a motel.

"Thank you so much," he told Santa.

Steve Gladney, the Highway Patrol lieutenant, grinned as he watched.

"I've been in the Highway Patrol a lot of years and seen and done a lot of things," he said. "But this is the highlight of my career. I'm glad there's someone like him who doesn't forget where he came from."

His co-worker, Staff Sgt. Scott Swanson, felt he'd experienced the true meaning of Christmas.

"Everything's gotten so commercial," Scott said. "This brings it back to what it's all about."

Santa still had a little money lingering in his pocket, so on the way to the airport, he stopped at a Coleman's Barbecue in Hernando, Mississippi. After eating, he handed Dick money for each of the employees. Dick walked behind the front counter and handed it out.

"This is a miracle," one recipient said.

"I want to cry," said another.

Some weeks later, Santa heard that those folks still were talking about the money.

Thirty-six

Two prayers

A homeless woman named Tammy prayed for a successful overnight shift as she drove to work at an Independence restaurant three days before Christmas.

She and her husband, Dave, needed help.

"God," she said, "I firmly believe you help those who help themselves."

Previously, while living in North Carolina, Tammy and Dave had earned a combined $65,000 a year. Tammy managed a restaurant, where she toiled 70 hours a week. Dave was a chef, a trade he learned in school.

Then Dave's manager laid him off. Tired of long hours, Tammy agreed she needed a change, too. They decided to move to Nevada, where one of Dave's former teachers promised to help Dave find work. They sold some of their belongings and loaded the rest into their car.

On the way west, a hit-and-run driver sideswiped them. They spent $1,800 just to make the car drivable again. After reaching western Missouri, they ran out of gas and money, so they slept several November nights in their car.

Sunday morning, they walked into Mass at St. John LaLande Catholic Church in Blue Springs. As they left, the priest asked who they were. Dave explained what had happened.

The church bought them a tank of gas, provided two nights in a motel and gave them contact numbers for City Union Mission, a Kansas City agency that operates faith-based homeless shelters, including one for families.

Tammy and Dave moved into the shelter and looked for work
— their way back to stability. Shelter officials said they could stay for
a month.

After three weeks, they had saved enough for rent. The day they
were to meet with their new landlord, their car broke down. Repairs
took $240. Tammy grabbed extra shifts at the restaurant, working as
much as 14 hours a day, to help make up the lost money. They re-
scheduled a meeting with their landlord for December 23, three days
before their stay at the shelter was to end.

December 22, Tammy headed to work for a 13-hour shift knowing that they probably would be short of cash the next day. She feared
that since they didn't have local references, the landlord wouldn't
accept their being short.

She had asked two other waitresses for money, but it was Christ-
mastime, and they needed everything they had. She asked her boss
for an advance, but he said no. She hadn't told them that she and
Dave were homeless.

So she prayed.

Shortly before her shift ended the next morning, she ducked into
the restroom and counted her tips. Her heart sank. She needed $40
more. Dave would be picking her up soon, and they were short.

"God," she prayed, "I know I'm still short, but I'll ask the landlord…"

Three more customers came in the front door. Tammy grabbed
menus and decided to serve them, even though three meals probably wouldn't generate enough tip money. She already had logged 42
hours that week, with three shifts to go.

One customer studied the menu for something low in carbohy-
drates but didn't see anything.

"You need one of our low-carb menus," Tammy said, grabbing one
from another table. She poured Santa some coffee.

Santa had awakened at 3:46 a.m. After praying for his own
"special gift" from God, he checked his e-mails, pondered the great
week he'd already had and decided to get breakfast. He drove toward

a favorite restaurant but when he reached a nearby stoplight, something prompted him to make a U-turn. He pulled onto an interstate ramp and drove.

About 5:30 a.m., he pulled off to try First Watch. The windows were dark. He turned around in the parking lot and thought about settling for a fast-food breakfast sandwich. Then he remembered that a friend had mentioned an IHOP not far away with free Internet access. He didn't have his laptop with him, but the restaurant might be worth checking out. He headed east and found the IHOP tucked behind a Wendy's.

A pleasant woman gave him a non-smoking table and waited on him warmly, as if she had been there for years. After bringing his food, Tammy checked often to see if he needed anything else.

After Santa finished, Tammy delivered his bill for $9.10.

"Pay anytime," she said. "There's no rush."

Soon, she stopped at his table again.

"Do you need to close out?" Santa asked.

"How did you know that?" Tammy asked, laughing. Dave was waiting.

Santa reached in his pocket and pulled out $100.

"Oh, I'll cover the 10 cents," Tammy said.

"I've got a dime," Santa said, and they both laughed. Tammy went for his change and came back with a handful.

Santa asked if she had read about that man in the paper who gave out hundred-dollar bills. Tammy shook her head. She hadn't seen the paper.

"I've always wanted to do that," Santa said, "so I had decided that the first person I came in contact with this morning, I was going to say, 'Keep the change.' "

He looked at her and repeated the words: "Keep the change."

Tears formed in the corners of her eyes. She hugged Santa.

"Sir, you have no idea — no idea!"

She told him about being homeless, about needing $40 more in tips to pay for an apartment, about praying for help.

"My prayers have been answered," Tammy said, crying. "You're an angel."

Santa barely reached the parking lot before he broke down in the early-morning darkness. He thanked God for the marvelous gift then fished in his pockets until he found two more hundred-dollar bills.

He walked back inside, spotted Tammy wiping away tears and slipped the extra money into her hand. She tried to wave him off, even though she and Dave had no furniture and could use the money for an air mattress and a small television in their new apartment. Everything that had happened to them in Jackson County had been such a blessing that they had decided to make this their new home. And though God had been in their lives before, they felt closer to him now, more spiritual than ever, because of all the kindness others had bestowed.

Now, a stranger was saving them again. And Tammy was crying again.

"Sir, you don't have to do that," she told Santa, who insisted she take the cash.

He hugged her and whispered into her ear.

"That's just what I do."

Thirty-seven

'Can you keep a secret?'

S anta sauntered into Town Topic and took a seat on one of its stools. Bonnie stood behind the counter, alongside a waitress named Patty. Santa chatted with them a bit, asking about their health and other topics.

Then he mentioned the man who gave away money each year.

"I work for that guy," Santa said. "He told me to stop by."

He handed each woman $100. Patty began trembling. "Now I just need $13 more to pay my gas bill," she said.

Santa handed each of them another $100. Patty gasped.

Bonnie told him about the time Santa came in and ordered food from her, but she didn't know it was him.

"I sure wish I would have known," she said.

Santa looked her in the eyes.

"Can you keep a secret?" he asked.

"I can always keep a secret."

"You want to thank that guy?"

Bonnie nodded.

"You just did," Santa said.

Bonnie started to cry. She came out from behind the counter and gave Santa a big hug.

"Thank you," she said.

SANTA'S SECRET: A STORY OF HOPE

Thirty-eight

Bad news

Several days after visiting Bonnie, Santa picked up a to-go order from an oriental restaurant and headed home. As he ate, he felt food stacking in his throat. He couldn't swallow, so he vomited.

That was strange, he thought.

A few weeks later, he stopped at Cracker Barrel for some turnip greens and cornbread. Once again, his meal caught in his throat. He ducked into the restroom and vomited.

Later, he told a friend what happened.

"That sounds like a hiatal hernia," said the friend. A large hiatal hernia where the food pipe joins the stomach could cause food to back up.

Santa made a mental note to schedule a doctor's visit, but family issues and a sick relative distracted him. Weeks passed. When he told his doctor in early April his problem, the doctor immediately sent Santa for tests. A throat scope illuminated a golf-ball-sized mass in his esophagus.

"It looks malignant," said the gastroenterologist, who took a biopsy.

Malignant?

Doctors now wanted CT scans of Santa's chest, abdomen and pelvis.

"How's the day after tomorrow?" the scheduler asked Santa. In a daze, he nodded. He had figured his problem was caused by acid reflux or a hernia. He never expected this.

Two mornings later, he awoke early. Opening his journal, he jotted: *Today I find out if I have cancer. I'm scared and kind of numb. I pray to God for good news....*

He thought about friends who had battled cancer. Some had lost. One was fighting a recurrence of prostate cancer. Santa's sister, Elizabeth, had defeated what doctors had called terminal breast cancer 10 years earlier. She had told Santa that the M.D. Anderson Cancer Center in Houston offered the nation's best treatment, if that's what he needed. Others recommended the Mayo Clinic in Minnesota.

A few hours after finishing his CT scans at St. Luke's Hospital, Santa's cell phone rang as he drove through a Kansas City suburb.

"You have cancer," his doctor reported.

Shaking, Santa pulled over and called the love of his life.

"I'm so sorry," he told her. They both cried. "It could be worse," he said. "It could be one of the kids. I am glad it's me and not one of you."

Later that day, more bad news came by phone. The cancer had spread to a lung and his liver.

Santa told one of his brothers-in-law.

"If anyone can beat this, you can — and you will," the brother-in-law said.

Santa talked with Elizabeth several times that day, leaning on her both for comfort and hope. She promised to help. Knowing that she defeated cancer, and that she shared his genes, helped some.

That evening, one of his sons called. Choking back tears, Santa broke the news.

"I love you, Dad," his son said.

§ § §

Unsure what to blame for the cancer, Santa read all he could about healthy diets and special food. He threw out his nonstick cookware and bought stainless steel. He tried to force himself to eat, but his appetite, which already had waned, now vanished.

A few days after being diagnosed, he awoke with pain in his right side. It felt like a pulled muscle but he knew it wasn't. He remembered feeling a similar pain in March, but it went away. Why hadn't he gone to the doctor then?

He opened his journal. *I have a lot of guilt looking back, knowing I could have taken better care of myself. I've been beating myself up....*

A friend recommended he live every minute to the fullest. He agreed, but he felt that would be hard to do until he learned more about what he faced. Was his cancer curable? He didn't know, but what he read on the Internet worried him. Five-year survival rates were low.

He told one friend that he felt undeserving of his financial success and all the friends rallying around him. The friend answered, "If there is one man deserving, it is you."

Santa began researching his health insurance plan, doctors and hospitals. He opened the journal again. Writing, which his son had recommended, seemed to help.

My biggest fear of dying is not for me, it's for my family. I hope to see some grandchildren someday. Elizabeth pointed out that's a good reason to live and fight this thing. When a doctor tells someone they have six months or a year to live, it seems to come true. I believe that the patient believes it and the body starts to shut down. Elizabeth said that's exactly what her first doctors told her.

Elizabeth had refused to die. She couldn't leave her two little boys without a mother. He could learn from her determination.

I've come face to face with mortality, and I'm not as scared as I always thought I would be if I was told I had a life-threatening illness. Crap, I don't even have a will yet. For some reason, I thought it was bad luck. I can't do that to my family. I will start the process today... I'm sure the next six to eight months are going to be a roller coaster ride... I'm going to live every moment to its fullest, tell lots of people I love them. I'm going to get on as many prayer lists as I can.

The pain in his right side nagged him, especially when he breathed deeply. He wished it would go away. He wished he could sleep through the night, instead of waking every two or three hours. No wonder he felt so tired.

He thought back to when he smoked two and later three packs of cigarettes a day. He had quit 15 years ago but still enjoyed an occasional cigar. Could the tobacco be to blame? How about his diet? Though he'd been dieting for a few months, he'd made bad food choices for years and had grown obese. He chided himself for becoming a walking time bomb.

A week after being diagnosed, he sat on his back patio, waiting for the sunrise as the spring breeze brushed his face. Birds sang. He forced himself to eat a bowl of cereal and a banana. He opened his journal and noted that he had scheduled an appointment to set up a trust, make a will and write a health care directive. He also had read the pathology reports closer. The cancer was widespread in his liver, but the report didn't mention his lungs. Maybe the radiologist had been wrong. He hoped so.

He made an appointment with a local oncologist. Meanwhile, he asked others for advice. More people recommended M.D. Anderson, part of the University of Texas. Santa decided that's where he wanted to be treated, but he fretted about a possible waiting list. Thousands of cancer patients probably wanted help there, he reasoned. Could he get in?

He picked up the phone and called George Brett.

"I've got cancer and it doesn't look good," Santa said.

He asked George where his brother, Ken, had been treated for his cancer and then asked if George had any connections at M.D. Anderson. George didn't know anything about the facility or if it was difficult to be accepted as a patient there.

"I'll make a call," George said. He could tell Santa was frightened.

George dialed a friend, who called a friend. Soon, George called Santa back.

"Good things happen to good people," George told him. "Here's the number to call. Get on a plane."

Santa relayed the good news to family and friends. He put on a brave face while telling one: "I realize I have the fight of my life on my hands. Failure is not an option." He also talked of his faith in God. But inside, he remained tied in knots, full of doubt and fearing funerals.

His sister accompanied him to the local oncologist, who studied Santa's CT slides and confirmed that the esophageal cancer cells had spread to his liver.

"What about my lungs?" Santa asked.

"Your lungs? There's nothing in your lungs."

"What? They said it was in my lungs."

"I don't see a thing."

Santa exhaled. That was one bit of good news, anyway.

"What do you recommend I do?" Santa asked.

"If it were me, I'd go to M.D. Anderson," the oncologist said.

Santa nodded. He had an appointment.

"Go," the oncologist said. "That's the best place in the world. I work with them, and I'd be glad to work with them through this."

§ § §

A few days before his flight to Houston, Santa awoke with worse pain in his abdomen. It intensified as the day progressed. By Friday, it felt excruciating. His doctor provided a prescription for Fentanyl patches. He tried putting one on, but it wouldn't stick. Ray Wynn taped it for him.

Later, Santa wrote in his journal: *I'm scared, very scared, still in shock, hoping this is just a long dream and I will wake up and everything is okay, but I know it's not. This is as real as it gets, folks... I know every-one ever born is going to die sometime. None of us knows when. At least if I do die from this illness, it's given me time to prepare and get things in order so I don't have to leave a mess for my family.*

One of Santa's sons flew to Houston with Santa for the first of many visits to M.D. Anderson. As he walked in the main doors, Santa instantly felt calmer, as if sensing he'd come to the right place. Maybe someone above was trying to tell him everything would be okay.

His "advocate" introduced herself and guided him through the facility. His new doctor described his type of cancer as incurable, inoperable but treatable. They'd know more after running more tests.

The words bounced through Santa's head. *Incurable. Inoperable. Treatable.*

Another of Santa's sons flew to Houston to join them. So did Larry McCormick, the retired FBI agent. Santa underwent more CT scans and other tests before being sent home. He'd have to wait about 10 days for the results.

Back in Missouri, his stomach pain increased. The pain patch wasn't helping as much as he hoped.

§ § §

Ten days later, he sat in the doctor's office in Houston, waiting for the confirmation that he dreaded. He knew what to expect, but the words still hurt.

Tests confirmed that he had Stage IV esophageal cancer, the most advanced form. Esophageal cancer often was diagnosed late, his doctor explained, because symptoms seldom appeared before the cancer entered Stage III or IV.

Officially, his cancer was adenocarcinoma, which typically starts in the lower esophagus, near the stomach. Most experts believe it grows after acid reflux damages tissue there. Santa's case was so far advanced that if he had waited four weeks longer, his liver would have failed.

The cancer was spreading rapidly, his doctor explained. Already, the tumors were larger than they had been when he took his CT scans back in Missouri. She wanted to aggressively fight back. Did Santa want to fight?

"Yes," he said.

M.D. Anderson was participating in a clinical trial of a three-drug combination that had shown great promise for shrinking his type of cancer, though there was no guarantee it would help him, the doctor said. Fifty-one patients were being accepted. Did Santa want to participate, if he was eligible?

Hope crept into Santa's mind. He brightened.

"You bet!" he said.

More tests followed. If the liver lesions had advanced too far, he would be ineligible. As Santa waited in an exam room for an answer, he prayed for good news. Finally, the door handle turned. A nurse stuck her head inside, smiled and held up a thumb. Santa could participate.

A packet of materials explained the study, the drugs used and other issues. Possible side effects included nausea, hair loss, fatigue, unsteadiness, tingling in the fingers and many other discomforts. He'd need blood drawn before every treatment. If the cancer grew, or he could not tolerate the side effects, he would be taken off the trial. Most patients, though, tolerated the drugs well and even continued to work between treatments, the doctor said.

The informed consent form ran for nine pages. Santa signed.

He already had checked into Rotary House, a hotel connected to M.D. Anderson by enclosed walkways. He had a bedroom, small bathroom and a living area with a fridge and dishwasher. He bought bottled water by the case and stocked the fridge.

It would be a few days before his first round of chemotherapy. If everything went well, he'd receive a treatment every other weekend for 24 weeks. After every four treatments, the hospital would take new CT scans to see how the cancer was reacting. The goal, his doctor said, was to shrink it and put it to sleep.

Two days before his first treatment, Santa awoke with a start. He opened his journal and wrote about a funeral procession he had pictured. Babe, the old plow horse his grandfather got in a trade, was pulling a wagon carrying Santa's simple pine box coffin. As they approached Santa's house in Missouri, Babe stopped so the pine box could be transferred into a limousine, which drove away. Before it reached the cemetery, the limousine stopped, and Babe took over again.

That strange procession reflected the phases in Santa's life, from poor boy to rich man to can't-take-it-with-you cancer victim. Santa's hand shook as he wrote about it.

The next day, he stood at his window, staring at shifting clouds. They reminded him how much fun it was as a child to look for animals or monsters in the clouds. As he watched, he saw an angel — not in the clouds but in a clear space between them. He turned and grabbed his camera phone to take a picture, but when he looked back, the angel had vanished. The clouds kept moving. Something resembling Satan's head formed, only to be crushed as the clouds shifted. What did it mean? Santa backed away from the window.

Friends and family bought airline tickets and rotated into Houston to keep Santa company.

Saturday arrived. Santa walked into a private treatment room where he could watch television while the drugs entered his veins through a catheter a nurse had placed in his left arm the previous day.

One of the drugs, Oxaliplatin, was a chemotherapy drug that interfered with DNA. It would take two hours to infuse. Another drug, docetaxel, interfered with cell division. It would take one hour to infuse.

The third drug, 5-FU, was a chemotherapy drug that interfered with cell metabolism. A continuous 24-hour portable pump — about the size of a Sony Walkman — would pump it into Santa's vein for 48 hours.

After about five hours in the treatment room, he would leave and carry the pump in a fanny pack, making sure not to kink the tubing that ran from the pump to his left arm. He was told not to drink or touch anything cold for five days because of the bad reaction it could cause.

The first treatment ended uneventfully.

Two days later, Santa grew mildly nauseated. He grabbed his anti-nausea medicine, just in case.

Three days later, he awoke at 2:30 a.m. with diarrhea, one of the side effects about which he had been forewarned. Within hours, he made five more trips to the bathroom.

By now, he'd dropped 50 pounds, and his waistline continued to shrink. Loose skin hung from his neck.

Santa felt like he had told his story a thousand times — to friends, to doctors, to nurses, to strangers. He began thinking about the future and pondered what God wanted him to do. He pictured himself giving testimony about the joy of giving, the power of hope and how Christ had worked in his life.

His grace is without boundaries, Santa wrote in his journal. *My faith does get stronger… I've been praying about how I can serve the Lord. There's lots to think about. First things first. Let's get this cancer in remission.*

In mid-May, he showed his "advocate," a registered nurse, his pain patch and asked if he had it on right. She laughed.

"It's on backward!"

Santa groaned. For about three weeks, he'd been wearing all of his patches backward, getting no benefit at all. His advocate turned the patch around. Soon, Santa started feeling a buzz. The next day, he called his nurse.

"Take it off," the nurse said. "You don't need it."

A few days later, he gave blood for more tests, which showed that his white blood cells hadn't bounced back fast enough from the chemotherapy.

"You'll have to wait one more week," the nurse said. "Don't worry. This happens."

It was a small setback. But Santa was regaining some appetite and his skin color had improved. One of his sons had arrived to spend infusion day with him. Now, they spent a free day together instead. The delay meant that Cecil, who was planning a Memorial Day weekend visit, would be there to keep him company for Round 2.

One morning, Santa noticed that some of his white hair was falling out. Deciding to get it over with, he walked to the M.D. Anderson beauty shop and asked for his head to be shaved. He covered his baldness with a new ball cap — a Texas Longhorns cap.

Santa picked up Cecil at the airport. When infusion time arrived, Cecil took a chair next to Santa's cot and began to watch the television in the private infusion room. A nurse hooked up Santa's meds and left. Within minutes, Santa felt a stinging pain in his back. His skin reddened. He could hardly breathe. His chest hurt.

Cecil ran for the nurse, who injected an allergy medicine into Santa's I.V. fluid bag and began pumping the bag by hand.

"Why are you squeezing it?" Cecil asked.

"To get it in there quick," the nurse said.

The pain ebbed. Santa's nurse told him not to worry. This happens sometimes.

Later, Santa and Cecil checked his treatment paperwork for warnings about infusion side effects.

Please notify your chemotherapy nurse for signs of allergic reaction: red flushed face within the first five minutes of infusion, a heavy feeling in the chest within the first five minutes, lower pack pain… a hot flash…

Santa had experienced them all.

§ § §

As the doctors predicted, Santa felt good enough between treatments to work on his laptop, take walks and go out for meals. So, after a month away, he flew home.

It felt good to spin through familiar neighborhoods and see familiar landmarks. He talked to his pastor, visited his in-laws and caught up on goings-on.

"There's no place like home," he said, like Dorothy from "The Wizard of Oz."

As he drove along Interstate 70, he noticed two hitchhikers standing on the shoulder. After he passed, a strange feeling hit. *Wait,* he thought. *I was supposed to stop.* He exited at the next ramp, found a bank, withdrew money from an automated teller machine and circled back to I-70.

The couple still stood on the shoulder, waiting. Santa pulled over.

They ran to his car.

"My boss sent me here," Santa said.

The hitchhikers were headed to Denver to see their daughter, they said. They had stopped earlier at an Odessa church, and a man had given them fried chicken.

Santa asked if they had been praying. The man looked at his wife.

"Honey, remember 10 minutes ago, when I said we was going to get a miracle, that we'd get a ride?"

She nodded.

Santa smiled. He reached under his leg, where he had hidden $300 in twenty-dollar bills, the denomination the ATM had provided. He gave them the cash. The man stared. The woman bawled.

"What's your name?" the man asked.

"Bubba," Santa said.

He drove them to the bus station in Kansas City. They thanked him and promised to pray for him.

The next day, Santa headed to the airport for another flight to Houston.

§ § §

After four rounds of chemotherapy, his doctors scheduled Santa for new CT scans. What had happened to the monster inside him? Were the drugs working?

"You'll know before we will," the medical folks told Santa.

He felt better. He wasn't having any trouble swallowing food. Perhaps the drugs were working. He'd learn the results two days after the scans, on July 5.

Santa awoke that morning, crawled out of bed and got down on his knees. It had been 90 days since his diagnosis.

"God, I pray for a miracle today, I pray for good news today. I need good news today. That's what I want. It's in your hands, and I trust you."

Santa arrived for his 1:30 p.m. doctor's appointment, nervous yet eager to learn the test results. Larry McCormick sat with him. After a half hour, a nurse called Santa's name. She took his blood pressure and temperature and checked his weight — then Santa had to wait some more. He looked out a window, saw clouds and told Larry, "I need good news on a cloudy day." Larry laughed. "Sounds like a song title."

Santa closed his eyes and said another prayer. He felt calm yet worried. What if he got a bad report? What then?

Two of the doctor's assistants arrived first and said the doctor was running late. One of the assistants noticed Santa's nervousness.

"I can't let you sit there like this," he said. "We've got good news for you, but the doctor wants to tell you."

Santa's eyes watered. He tried to stop the tears, but he couldn't.

The doctor arrived.

"You did great," she said. "I'm going to pull up the CT scans and I'm going to show you the difference."

She put his old scans alongside the new ones. Santa glanced back and forth. The difference was obvious. The doctor explained how they measured the lesions. His largest liver tumor was half the size it had been two months earlier. His liver functions were nearly back to normal.

"You've had no trouble swallowing, have you," the doctor asked, already knowing the answer.

They talked longer, as Santa fought to hold back his emotions. Silently, he offered prayers of thanks. The doctor explained that of 31 participants in the study, 29 had shown the same kind of results. Because of the remarkable results, the study would be expanded to 80 people.

Finally she told him that if he wanted to celebrate, he could have a glass of wine. He begged off, saying that alcohol would stress his liver.

"Okay," the doctor said. "Your next treatment is Saturday, and you are good to go."

Santa returned to his room. Outside, the clouds had vanished, leaving a sparkling blue sky. Santa needed to take Larry to the airport soon, but first, he wanted to let his friends know how well things had gone. He turned on his laptop and sent a group e-mail reporting the good news. He added: *From the bottom of my heart, I thank you for all your prayers. Keep 'em coming. Prayer is the difference.*

Later that day, Sheriff Tom called. Other friends called. Santa's phone rang and rang.

"It was just a blessed day today," he told them. "I am so grateful."

§ § §

After four more treatments over eight weeks, Santa repeated his CT scans and returned to the doctor's office to again learn the results. Once again, the news was good. All the lesions had shrunk even further — and by double-digit percentages.

Back home between treatments, Santa pulled on a yellow shirt, the color worn by cancer survivors. Some of his white hair had grown back. He'd traded the Texas ball cap for a navy one with a pink Superman's emblem in the middle. JESUS was written across the Superman emblem. The words "Super Jesus" were embroidered along the left side of the cap's bill. Santa drove to the city market and bought more of the caps to share with friends.

§ § §

In September, he took a call from a friend of Buck O'Neil, the former Negro League baseball player whom Kansas Citians had championed for the Baseball Hall of Fame. A special committee had selected other former Negro League players earlier that year but left out Buck, who graciously accepted the news and still agreed to speak at the induction ceremony. Now, weeks after that ceremony, Buck was in the hospital for the second time. News reports blamed exhaustion, but Buck had cancer, and it was in his bone marrow. He had asked his friends to keep this a secret.

"Buck wants to see you," the caller told Santa.

Santa drove to the hospital, remembering how he and Buck had met when they were paired at a charity golf tournament many years earlier. Buck's love-of-life demeanor had won over Santa immediately.

When he walked in Buck's hospital room, Santa was stunned by how frail and unlike himself Buck looked. They talked. Santa offered encouragement. Buck reminded Santa that Santa had promised to speak at Buck's church. Santa said he still would, as long as Buck would speak at his. Buck grinned. "All right," he said.

As Santa stood to leave, he reached for Buck's hand.

"Uh uh," Buck said, shaking his head. He opened his arms. "Give me some!"

Santa leaned down for a hug.

About two weeks later, the night before Santa's next-to-last chemotherapy treatment, Santa's phone rang in Houston. It was Evelyn Belser, a close friend of Buck's who had stayed at Buck's hospital bedside for weeks. She tearfully told Santa that Buck had passed less than an hour earlier. Santa's heart sank. He'd prayed for Buck to make it, though he knew how seriously ill his friend had been.

Shaking, Santa called a friend back in Missouri.

"We lost Buck," he reported, trying not to cry. He swallowed. "You think you are prepared for it, but you never are."

His mind flashed back to all the wonderful moments shared with Buck and some of the great one-liners the gentle giant had unleashed. Buck talked about hating cancer because it took his wife and hating AIDS because it took other people's lives. "But I can't hate another human being," Buck had said, "because we are all God's children."

Then there was the time he watched Buck cajole an audience to stand and sing. Buck sang a phrase first and had the audience repeat it. *The greatest thing… in all my life… is loving you…*

If only more people were like Buck.

Santa sighed.

"It looks like Buck's name will be on a lot of hundred-dollar bills this year," he said.

Thirty-nine

What next?

Pundits say that battling a life-threatening illness changes a person. For Santa, that certainly has been true — and not just because he thinks more about his faith, his family and the need to tell others how much they mean to him, before he loses the chance.

Battling cancer also has prompted him to re-examine his future as Kansas City's most famous anonymous giver.

Perhaps, he says, it is time to pass the baton to other Secret Santas. Let them give away money at Christmas. He'll retire and coach instead, training others to find targets and also stay safe while carrying cash.

Perhaps he'll climb in his car and travel America's dusty roads to tell his story to church groups, hospital patients and others who need to hear about the power of faith, hope and charitable giving.

And perhaps he'll reveal his identity, so that he can better explain his story without worrying that someone will attend his speaking engagement with a hidden camera, just to get a picture and "out" him without his permission.

But if he does spill the secret, and the Santa mystery ends, will others actually take over and keep the tradition alive?

As Santa ponders these questions and others, he hopes that people who read his story remember this important message: Life should be about giving. And you don't need copious cash to do it well. You can give of yourself.

"Every day, I make sure that before I lay my head down on my pillow to go to sleep, I make sure that I have done one good thing that day, just one," Santa explained.

He continually looks for opportunities to be nice, even in small ways, whether by opening a door or pushing someone's grocery cart back to the store.

"Instead of ignoring the person standing outside in the hallway, waiting to clean a restroom, instead of walking by and acting as if they don't exist, say something meaningful to them," he said. "If you do this, you find yourself looking for ways to make someone's day a little better. It doesn't hurt to say: 'Hello. How are you today?' "

He paused.

"I've got this vision that I wake up with. It's called 'One K,' and One K equals one act of kindness today. Do one K a day. Just one K."

If everyone did that, he said, it would be "kinda cool."

Several years ago, Santa posted a four-part mission on his website. He wanted to show by example that a simple, single act of kindness can change an individual's life forever. He wanted to urge others to give without the expectation of anything in return. He wanted to show how to have an impact in the community. And he wanted to create a worldwide network of Secret Santas.

There may not be a worldwide network yet, but Santa has trained two Kansas residents to be Santas.

In 2004, the new Miami County Santa — also known by the code name Noble Smith — accompanied Santa on a jaunt through downtrodden neighborhoods. He experienced a "jumper," a recipient so thrilled that she jumped and jumped in glee. The 50-year-old homeless woman dropped both bags she was carrying when the Miami County Santa waved $100 in front of her on Independence Avenue. She hugged him then hugged Secret Santa, who offered a second bill.

"Oh my God!" Alice Lowder exclaimed. "Oh God! Thank you Jesus! Oh Lordy! Awwwwww!"

She jumped again, cried, thanked the men and cried some more. Somehow, she ended up with $300. Jumpers have a way of getting extra money out of Santa. They also inspire the new Santas, who are amazed at the reaction $100 or $200 or $300 given by a stranger can generate.

In 2005, Noble Smith joined Santa again, and Santa recruited another Santa-in-training, this one from Johnson County, Kansas. The newest trainee experienced a "swooner," as recipients are called when they swoon to the floor inside a thrift shop or other store.

The newest Santa also learned about locating targets when Santa took her to a grocery store parking lot.

"What are we doing here?" she asked, perplexed because people coming out with groceries obviously had money to spend. She soon found, though, that many were spending the last of their paycheck or disability check on food for their Christmas dinner. Santa knew that simply by knowing the neighborhood near the grocery store.

Along the years, a growing number of elves have learned Santa's tricks, too. Following him is a special experience, for many reasons, they say.

"It isn't necessarily the amount he gives," said Carl Tripp, one of the firefighter elves. "It's the total generosity, it's the total kindness. It seeing people react when somebody gave them something just to be nice to them."

For Susan Tvedten, watching Santa work is "awesome."

"He actually has strategies for finding the neediest people," she said. "That impressed me. He wasn't just going around and picking a street…. And he looks at people's shoes. That's the coolest thing."

How much longer will the elves revel in the glow of Santa's kindness? As this is being written, Santa is contemplating one long sleigh ride in December, possibly to two large U.S. cities before finishing back home, once again spreading hundred-dollar bills through Kansas City streets.

Then it will be time to change direction, he says.

"My new calling is to go and talk to anybody who will listen, and to bring them the message of hope," he said.

There's always hope, he says — no matter your background, no matter the circumstances in which you were raised, no matter your current environment, no matter the obstacles you face, including life-threatening illnesses.

"I also want to share where I draw my strength from — and that's from God," he said. "I find that when I seek God's counsel and I follow his guidance, life is a breeze."

Finally, he says, he wants to make the most of his second chance.

"So many people don't have a second chance," he said. "I've known people who have gotten killed in car wrecks or died instantly from heart attacks, and they didn't have the opportunity that I have — the opportunity to get right with the universe, to get right with God, to get right with people that I feel I may have wronged…

"That's my new mission, to pass on all the lessons I've learned throughout life. That it is more blessed to give than to receive. That the more that you give — not just of your resources, but of yourself, your time, a smile, listening with a kind heart — those are ways that you can contribute to mankind and make this a better world….

"While I'll still battle my daily battle with my illness, I've never been more at peace than at any other time in my life because no matter what God decides is in store for me, whether he says, 'I'm finished with you here on this earth,' or not, I'm going to be in a wonderful place either way.

"I may have cancer, my body may have cancer, but I've got Christ in my life."

MISSISSIPPI, 1958:
Santa, age 10, with his
grandparents in front of
an uncle's 1954 Chevy.
*(Photo courtesy of Santa's
sister, all rights reserved.)*

KANSAS CITY, 1971: Santa
climbed off a Greyhound bus as a
young salesman carrying $18 in his
pocket and everything he owned in
this small suitcase. *(Photo by author.
All rights reserved.)*

MISSISSIPPI, 1996: Mike Hailey
with the motorcycle Santa purchased.
Mike died in 2003. *(Photo courtesy of
George Hailey, all rights reserved.)*

MISSISSIPPI, 1980s: Ruby Horn in front of the Ted Horn Food Service truck. *(Photo courtesy of Ted Horn, all rights reserved.)*

TUPELO, Mississippi, 1999: Ted Horn, the retired owner of the Dixie Diner, accepts $10,000 during a surprise visit from Secret Santa, who thanked Ted for rescuing him with $20 in 1971. *(Photo courtesy of The Kansas City Star, copyright 1999, all rights reserved.)*

NEW YORK, 2001: When this store reopened two months after 9/11, it preserved history in its front display case. Thick dust still covered the clothes. *(Photo courtesy of Ray Wynn, all rights reserved.)*

NEW YORK, 2001: By the time Secret Santa visited, workers already had removed most of the above-ground debris from Ground Zero. Large cranes helped them continue to dig out what was compacted below street level, in a hole where the World Trade Center towers once stood. *(Photo courtesy of Ray Wynn, all rights reserved.)*

NEW YORK, 2001: Outside a fire station on lower Manhattan, Santa studies a memorial honoring 14 of the station's firefighters. *(Photo courtesy of The Kansas City Star, copyright 2001, all rights reserved.)*

NEW YORK, 2001: Observers study the many notes and other items posted outside St. Paul's Chapel, which served as a place of rest and refuge for Ground Zero workers. For eight months, volunteers working 12-hours shifts served meals and provided other services inside. *(Photo courtesy of Ray Wynn, all rights reserved.)*

NEW YORK, 2001: The Rev. Lyndon Harris talks with Santa in St. Paul's Chapel, which suffered very little damage when the nearby towers collapsed. Santa donated $5,000. *(Photo courtesy of The Kansas City Star, copyright 2001, all rights reserved.)*

NEW YORK, 2001: Outside the Episcopal chapel, messages run the length of the sidewalk. *(Photo courtesy of Ray Wynn, all rights reserved.)*

KANSAS CITY, 2001: Firefighters surprised Santa, making him cry, when they gave him this leather helmet and hand-painted shield inside a Kansas City fire station. *(Photos courtesy of the author, all rights reserved.)*

SOUTHERN CALIFORNIA, 2003: Steven and Pam Samson smile after receiving $300 apiece from Santa near where their home once stood in Crest. *(Photo courtesy of The Kansas City Star, copyright 2003, all rights reserved.)*

SOUTHERN CALIFORNIA, 2003: Carmen and Laman Sadler, married 50 years, cried after receiving $1,000 from Santa. A wildfire consumed their home. *(Photo courtesy of The Kansas City Star, copyright 2003, all rights reserved.)*

SOUTHERN CALIFORNIA, 2003: Ray Wynn talks to flower saleswoman Kathy Peters in El Cajon. Santa gave Kathy $400 for $185 worth of cut flowers then let Kathy keep the flowers, too. *(Photo courtesy of The Kansas City Star, copyright 2003, all rights reserved.)*

KANSAS CITY: Over the years, Santa has visited Town Topic many times. Waitress Bonnie Gooch considers him "my angel from heaven." *(Photo courtesy of the author, all rights reserved.)*

KANSAS CITY, January 2004: Firefighters help Tracy Brazelton load her belongings so she can move to a rented house. Tracy was on the verge of homelessness. Santa paid six months' rent for her. *(Photo courtesy of The Kansas City Star, copyright 2004, all rights reserved.)*

FLORIDA, 2004: Santa marked his hundred-dollar bills with these stamps while on the road in Florida. His good friend, Charlie Meyerson, had died days after Thanksgiving. *(Photo courtesy of the author, all rights reserved.)*

FLORIDA, 2004: (Above) Riding in a rented van, elves Dick Butkus and Ray Wynn help watch for "targets" for Santa the year four hurricanes struck Florida. (Left) Rookie elf L.D. Stewart takes a break near his million-dollar bus. *(Above photo courtesy of the author, all rights reserved. Left photo courtesy of Ray Wynn, all rights reserved.)*

FLORIDA, 2004: (Right) Maria Calvillo, the mother of seven children, looks skeptical as Santa hands her $100 in a Wauchula parking lot. (Below) She grinned after realizing the money was real — and hers to keep. *(Photos courtesy of the author, all rights reserved.)*

FLORIDA, 2004: Inside a coin-operated laundry, Santa hands a hundred-dollar bill to a man who wanted change to do his laundry. *(Photo courtesy of the author, all rights reserved.)*

FLORIDA, 2004: Bev Chapman chats with a homeless man named Roberto, who couldn't remember his last name. Santa gave him $100 after seeing him digging in a trash bin for soda cans. *(Photo courtesy of the author, all rights reserved.)*

FLORIDA, 2004: (Right) Sheriff's Deputy Maria Trevino encourages hurricane victim Frank Peterson, 92, to accept $1,000 from Santa. Hurricane Charley destroyed his house. (Below) In tears, Frank embraced Maria. *(Photo courtesy of the author, all rights reserved.)*

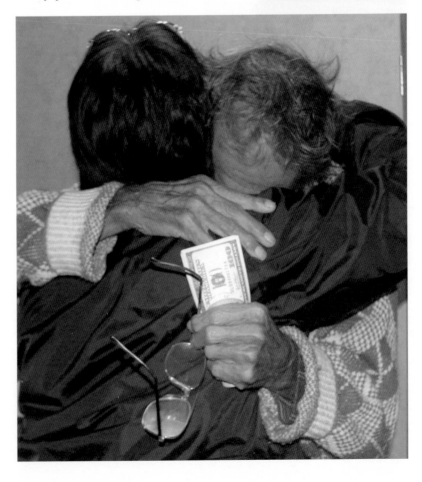

FLORIDA, 2004: Kenny Albritton, his wife, Merita, and their daughter, Zhaneta, study a hundred-dollar bill Santa handed them, before he gave them nine more bills. *(Photo courtesy of the author, all rights reserved.)*

FLORIDA, 2004: After helping Santa give away money, Deputy Maria Travino talks to *Kansas City Star* photographer Tammy Ljungblad. Jackson County Sheriff Tom Phillips stands nearby. *(Photo courtesy of the author, all rights reserved.)*

FLORIDA, 2004: Dick Butkus pretends that he needs to be frisked by Sgt. Jim Nichols, who poses with his police dog, Hex, in Port Charlotte before helping escort Santa. Many officers wanted to be photographed with Dick. *(Photo courtesy of the author, all rights reserved.)*

FLORIDA, 2004: Tim Twyman and Bev Chapman of KMBC Channel 9 in Kansas City use a battered trailer home in Port Charlotte as a backdrop for a news report about Santa's philanthropy. *(Photo courtesy of the author, all rights reserved.)*

FLORIDA, 2004: Ray Wynn stands near a street sign bent by Hurricane Charley as deputies, Santa and elves visit in a trailer park where two persons died. *(Photo courtesy of the author, all rights reserved.)*

FLORIDA, 2004: (Top) Santa talks to the Lublin siblings outside Port Charlotte Adventist School before swearing them in (above) as elves while Dick Butkus watches. In the back row are Sachar, 11, Elijah, 9, and Nordwanna, 16. In front are Aunel, 6, and Scheyanne, 7. Santa gave them $1,000. *(Photo courtesy of the author, all rights reserved.)*

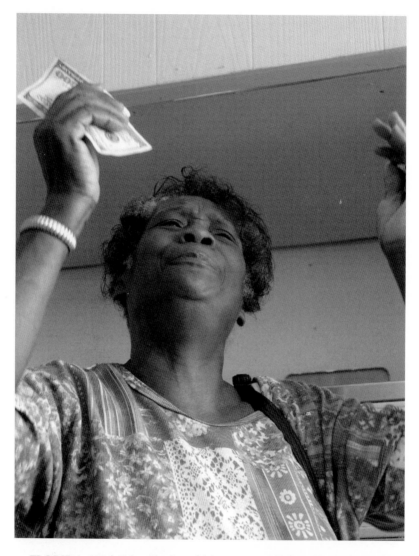

FLORIDA, 2004: Eslin Charlton celebrates getting $100 from Santa inside a coin-operated laundry. "Thank you, Jesus!" she exclaimed over and over. *(Photo courtesy of the author, all rights reserved.)*

FLORIDA, 2004: Pamela King, right, celebrates getting $300 with her sister-in-law, Raven Wilson, who received $100 from Santa. Pamela's sons, Matthew, 3, left, and Joseph, 4, accompanied them in Port Charlotte. *(Photo courtesy of the author, all rights reserved.)*

FLORIDA, 2004: Dick Butkus with Larry McCormick, who helped arrange security for several of Santa's trips and served as his driver. *(Photo courtesy of the author, all rights reserved.)*

FLORIDA, 2004: Mary Grimm of Port Charlotte couldn't believe it when Santa gave her $500 and handed money to her friend, too, outside a discount store. "I'll have to say a lot of prayers asking forgiveness for being mad at the Lord," she said. *(Photo courtesy of the author, all rights reserved.)*

FLORIDA, 2004: This young man had been reading a small bible when Santa spotted him outside a discount store in Port Charlotte. When Santa asked what he'd been reading, the man said it was 2 Corinthians, the part about how God likes a cheerful giver. Santa laughed and did some giving of his own. *(Photo courtesy of Ray Wynn, all rights reserved.)*

KANSAS CITY, 2004: Santa strums the guitar that firefighter Charlie Cashen gave him inside a fire station. *(Photo courtesy of the author, all rights reserved.)*

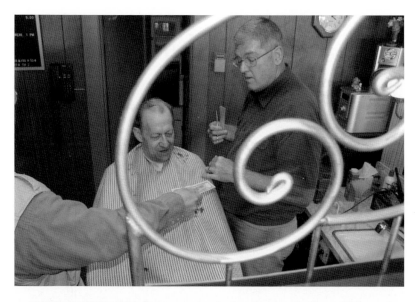

KANSAS CITY, 2004: Santa surprises barber shop owner Bryan Miller and customer Jerry Lawrence with $100 each. *(Photo courtesy of the author, all rights reserved.)*

KANSAS CITY, 2004: Michael Rash of Winona, Mississippi, grins while talking to Santa in the bus terminal. Santa gave him $300. *(Photo courtesy of the author, all rights reserved.)*

Cimeri Miller's ...

KANSAS CITY, 2004: Stranded in a bus terminal on Christmas Eve, Cimeri Miller wipes a tear after receiving $100. On the other end of the phone line, her husband waits to learn what is happening. (Facing page, top) After Santa adds $400, Cimeri cries some more. (Right) After he promises to buy her plane tickets home to California, she gleefully hugs her youngest son, Blake. *(Photos courtesy of the author, all rights reserved.)*

... Kansas City miracle

KANSAS CITY, 2004: Alice Lowder, a homeless woman, jumps for joy after two Santas — including one from Kansas being trained by Secret Santa — gave her money. *(Photo courtesy of The Kansas City Star, copyright 2004, all rights reserved.)*

KANSAS CITY, 2004: Santa surprises Seretta Taylor with $100 as she sits in her car outside the bus terminal. "Are you kidding?" she asked. She had just bought a bus ticket for a later trip. *(Photo courtesy of the author, all rights reserved.)*

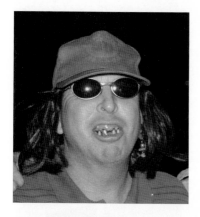

JACKSON, Mississippi, 2005: Cecil shows off the disguise he wore in 1998, when he and Santa attempted to hand out money in their hometown. *(Photo courtesy of the author, all rights reserved.)*

JACKSON, Mississippi, 2005: Dick Butkus and Ray Wynn outside Freddie's Restaurant, where Santa gave his elves matching Ben Hogan caps. Ray is weaing his backwards. *(Photo courtesy of the author, all rights reserved.)*

TUPELO, Mississippi, 2005:
Ted Horn helped Santa stamp bills
with Ted's name. *(Photo courtesy of*
the author, all rights reserved.)

TUPELO, Mississippi, 2005: Replaying their roles from 1971, Ted Horn
cooks breakfast for Santa, this time in Ted's kitchen. *(Photo courtesy of the author,*
all rights reserved.)

Ted Horn, left, and his son, David.

HOUSTON, Mississippi, 2005: Ted stands outside the former Dixie Diner, now a barber shop where haircuts cost $5. In 1971, a homeless and hungry Santa ordered breakfast here knowing he couldn't pay. *(All three photos courtesy of the author, all rights reserved.)*

WIGGINS, Mississippi, 2005: Jackson County Sheriff Tom Phillips consoles Wiggins Police Chief Buddy Bell. Santa gave $5,000 for families of two officers killed after responding to a domestic disturbance. *(Photo courtesy of the author, all rights reserved.)*

MISSISSIPPI, 2005: Genny Bohrer's children chant Ted Horn's name. Santa's former high school football coach, David Oakes, steered Santa to the family. *(Photo courtesy of the author, all rights reserved.)*

GULFPORT, Mississippi, 2005: Standing on a battered walkway along the beach, Ray Wynn admires the sunset. *(Photo courtesy of the author, all rights reserved.)*

GULFPORT, Mississippi, 2005: Across a highway from the beach, Ray Wynn takes pictures where a row of stately homes once stood. *(Photo courtesy of the author, all rights reserved.)*

JACKSON, Mississippi, 2005: (Below) Mayor Frank Melton, left, and FBI Special Agent in Charge John Raucci outside a YMCA day-care center where Santa donated $5,000. *(Photo courtesy of the author, all rights reserved.)*

JACKSON, Mississippi, 2005: (Above) After part-time dishwasher Joe Shanks promised to forward half of Santa's $100 gift to the Salvation Army, Santa handed him $400 more. *(Photo courtesy of the author, all rights reserved.)*

JACKSON, Mississippi, 2005: Christine McGee, right, and Carrie Richardson celebrate receiving $100 each in an outreach center's seamstress shop. "He helped us at a difficult time," Carrie said. *(Photo courtesy of the author, all rights reserved.)*

JACKSON, Mississippi, 2005: Stuart C. Irby Company workers examine cash handed out by Dick Butkus. Rodney Kendrick, seated, called his $100 a blessing. *(Photo courtesy of the author, all rights reserved.)*

NEAR MOUNT OLIVE, Mississippi, 2005: Angie Sullivan just happened to stop for gas at the same station where Santa stopped. He noticed the old truck she was filling and handed her $300. *(Photo courtesy of the author, all rights reserved.)*

KANSAS CITY, 2005:
Lisa Drome celebrates Santa's
gift as many others have,
with glee. *(Photo courtesy of*
The Kansas City Star, copyright
2005, all rights reserved.)

KANSAS CITY: John "Buck" O'Neil enjoyed playing
Santa's elf on several occasions. He died October 6, 2006.
(Photo courtesy of The Negro Leagues Baseball Museum, all
rights reserved.)